THE PREACHER
AND
HIS GREEK TESTAMENT

THE PREACHER
AND
HIS GREEK TESTAMENT

by

R. M. L. WAUGH, M.A., D.D.

with a Foreword by

J. ALEXANDER FINDLAY, M.A., D.D.

LONDON: THE EPWORTH PRESS

THE EPWORTH PRESS

(FRANK H. CUMBERS)

25-35 City Road, London, E.C.1.

MELBOURNE   CAPE TOWN
NEW YORK   TORONTO

Set in Monotype Baskerville 10 point
Made and printed in Great Britain by
William Clowes and Sons Ltd London and Beccles

To
MY WIFE

FOREWORD

by

Rev. J. Alexander Findlay, M.A., D.D.

As I greatly value the work Dr Waugh has put into this book, I am glad of the chance of recommending it to preachers of the Gospel who are anxious to keep up the Greek they learned at College and to use the original of the Greek Testament to the fullest advantage. It will help them to ply to and fro on the waters of Scripture. Moreover, it will enable them to build what my teacher, Rendel Harris, used to call 'railway-lines' in their Greek Testaments, to the very great advantage of their preaching. They will find it less necessary to fall back on the easy way out of exhortation—of which most congregations are heartily sick—to preach Christ rather than Christianity. Dr Waugh's book will, I feel sure, help toward this desirable result, and that is why I have real pleasure in recommending it.

PREFACE

Tennyson once expressed surprise at a preacher not being able to read the Bible in the original tongues. 'What,' said he, 'you the priest of a religion and you cannot read your own sacred books!' The Church does not expect all her ministers to be scholars, but she has a right to expect them to be scholarly. How tremendously important a thing it is that a preacher should be equipped to give a true exposition of a passage of Scripture!

Whilst the Hebrew language suffers less from translation than perhaps any other language, it is not so with a language like Greek which has a complex structure. A study of the marginal readings of the Revised Version is often very illuminating in this direction. Even an elementary knowledge of Greek with the use of a suitable dictionary can open a door through which the preacher can find suggestions for original sermons, guidance on the correct interpretation of puzzling texts, and delightful illustrations for his expositions.

John Wesley was an ardent evangelist; but it must not be forgotten that he was also a worthy scholar. In addition to writing over two hundred books and editing over one hundred others, he could quote from the Greek Testament even more exactly than from the Authorized Version. He revised the New Testament (with about 12,000 variations from the Authorized Version). At a particular time each day he and his brethren opened their Greek Testament to explore its riches. Having been a double Professor of Greek and of Logic in Lincoln College, Oxford, Wesley had great faith in a Church whose preachers were scholarly.

Writing of Thomas Walsh (one of the early Methodist preachers in Ireland), Wesley said: 'I know a young man who was so thoroughly acquainted with the Bible that if he was questioned concerning any Hebrew word in the Old, or any Greek word in the New Testament, he could tell after a little pause, not only how often the one or the other occurred in the

Bible, but also what it meant in every place.' Whilst the average minister may not excel in his linguistic studies he cannot but think seriously of Martin Luther's advice: 'Keep hard at the languages, for language is the sheath in which the sword of the Spirit rests.'

This book is written in answer to widespread requests from preachers who have read articles by the writer in religious papers such as *The Expository Times*, *The Christian World*, *The Preacher's and the Class-Leader's Magazine*, and *The Irish Christian Advocate*. Though much of the manuscript has had to be abbreviated in order to keep the publication reasonably cheap in these days of soaring prices, yet there is sufficient material in this book to stimulate interest and hope in the study of the New Testament. It is assumed that readers are in possession of a good grammar and lexicon.

My own interest was delightfully awakened when many years ago the Rev. David Smith, M.A., D.D., expounded a Greek word, about which I had written to him on a point of interpretation. Thereupon I purchased *The Vocabulary of the Greek New Testament* by Moulton and Milligan (Hodder & Stoughton). Acting on the suggestion of the late Rev. Wilbert F. Howard, M.A., D.D., F.B.A. (to whom I owe a very deep debt of gratitude for many kindnesses), I started to 'quarry' for the original meaning of Greek words. Much of the light discovered on the meaning of Greek words can be found in Moulton and Milligan's above cited book. In my general reading and in visits to university libraries the light of new knowledge that shone on old texts revealed a feast of good things for a hungry mind. It is some of this joy the writer of this book wishes to share with those whose knowledge of Greek has grown dim.

There is far too much topical preaching and superficial exhortation at the present time. A needy 'civilization' is waiting for some new panacea. The Church needs preachers who, like the Prophets of old, can proclaim a 'Thus saith the Lord'. If the preacher is to expound the Divine Revelation in Christ with authority and effectiveness he must give the most assiduous study to the Scriptures. May the publication of this book intensify his interest in this direction!

My sincere thanks is due to the Rev. J. Alexander Findlay, M.A., D.D., for the encouragement he has given me in pursuing my Greek studies. He has afforded some valuable suggestions regarding the contents of this book. His all too kind foreword to these studies is much appreciated. The writer is grateful to the Editors of *The Expository Times* and *Religion in Life* (an American Christian Quarterly) for their kind permission to use articles which recently appeared in their publications; to the Editors of *The Christian World*, and *The Irish Christian Advocate* for similar privileges; to Messrs Hodder & Stoughton and to Messrs Geoffrey Bles for permission to quote a few passages respectively from Moffatt's *New Translation* and from *Letters to Young Churches* (Phillips); also to Messrs T. & T. Clark for a few quotations from *A Companion to the Bible* (Manson); to Messrs Nisbet & Co. for some passages used from the book, *God and Man* (Farmer); to the Epworth Press for real help received from *The Bible Doctrine of Salvation* (C. Ryder Smith), *Jesus and His Church* (R. Newton Flew), and *Jesus and His Parables* (J. A. Findlay). Hastings' *Dictionary of the Bible* has also been of invaluable assistance.

May I warmly commend to young preachers A. T. Robertson's *Word Pictures in the New Testament* (Smith, New York), *The Moffatt New Testament Commentary* (Hodder & Stoughton), W. E. Vine's *Expository Dictionary of New Testament Words* (Oliphants), *The International Critical Commentary* (T. & T. Clark), *The Abingdon Commentary* (Epworth), and Trench's *New Testament Synonyms*. If I have overlooked acknowledging my indebtedness to any source not mentioned above, I offer my sincere apology. Unless where otherwise stated, the Revised Version is used throughout this book. In the Appendix will be found a list of the Greek words (nearly 260) which are discussed in these pages, and also the relevant Scripture citations.

I would express my gratitude to the Rev. S. J. W. Nabney, B.A., for revising the first edition, and to my son, Eric, for formulating the Indexes. Helpful suggestions from many readers have also been very much appreciated.

RICHARD M. L. WAUGH.

CONTENTS

PART THREE

THE STUDY OF THE WORD OF GOD   93

PART ONE

The Illumination of the Word of God *

A STUDY of the Greek New Testament is a delight to every lover of the Word of God. But to the preacher such a study is both a delight and a source of enrichment. What a strange thrill there is in discovering new light breaking forth from the sacred Scriptures! There is hardly a chapter in the New Testament that does not flash with a new glory when it is studied in the light of the new archaeological discoveries.

When the American troops were located for a while in Northern Ireland during the last War, they were welcomed as friends into many homes. It was a joy and privilege to have them. Just about that time the writer of this book made an interesting discovery. Paul uses a **verb** (ἐπισκηνόω: *episkeno-o*) in 2 Co 12₉ which the historian Polybius employed for the billeting of soldiers in private houses. Paul had been referring to 'a thorn in the flesh'; and in spite of this affliction he adds: 'Most gladly will I rather glory in my weaknesses, that the power of Christ may rest upon me' (ἐπισκηνώσῃ ἐπ' ἐμέ: *episkēnōse ep' eme*). Though the phrase can be translated 'spread a tabernacle over me', we are warranted in thinking that in our afflictions Christ with all His adequate resources and tender sympathy will come and make our hearts His home. We thereby experience what Von Hügel called 'an overflowing interior plenitude'.

There are *delicate shades of meaning* in the Greek original which will illuminate many a well-known passage. The very order of the Greek words is important. For instance, the writer of the Epistle to the Hebrews opens his treatise with the words, 'By divers portions and in divers manners' (πολυμερῶς καὶ πολυτρόπως: *polumerōs kai polutropos*), in order to give an

---

* The substance of this Chapter appeared in the March 1951 issue of *Religion in Life.*

added emphasis to the variety and imperfection of the earlier revelations, as contrasted with the complete and perfect revelation in Him who was God's own Son. Every detail in the text is worthy of careful examination.

To the reader of the English version the importance of a **prefix** or the **intensification of a verb** may not be apparent. Ἔρχομαι (*erchomai*), for example, has twelve different prefixes modifying the meaning 'come'. We are informed in Mk 10₂₁ that 'Jesus looking upon' the rich young ruler, 'loved him'. The Greek word here (ἐμβλέπω: *emblepō*) signifies 'looking into', or, as we would say, 'looking searchingly at'. It is the same word that is used about the maid of the High Priest who looked Peter up and down and remarked: 'Thou also wast with the Nazarene.' Jesus must have had wonderful eyes! Usually the Evangelists are silent about the appearance of their Master. It is, therefore, all the more significant that they refer several times to His looking at people, or looking round about Him. Mark has no less than three expressive words suggesting the sense of awe and wonder which filled the hearts of those who either listened to Christ's gracious words or gazed at His marvellous works.

Many Greek verbs are used in an intensified form, and this, too, must be observed. The treachery of Judas is clearly portrayed in the English words: 'And straightway he came to Jesus, and said, Hail, Rabbi; and kissed him' (Mt 26₄₉). But when we find that κατα (*kata*) is attached to φιλέω (*phileo*) with the meaning 'to kiss fervently' (RVm: 'kissed Him much'), and when we find in a papyrus that the same verb is used about a person who kissed the hand of another in a passion of gratitude (cf. also Lk 7₄₅), the treachery of Judas appears all the more despicable. Likewise, in the inimitable story of Jesus blessing the little children, we have an **intensive compound** employed. What a charming picture Mark gives us in his Gospel of our Lord, not only blessing (κατευλόγει: *kateulogei*) little children, but embracing (ἐναγκαλισάμενος: *enagkalisamenos*) them! (Mk 10₁₆). When Paul tells his Corinthian friends to 'attend upon the Lord without distraction' (1 Co 7₃₅) he uses a **compound** word—εὐπάρεδρος (*euparedros*)—which literally means 'sit well beside'. If the Comforter is to help us in our time of need, we must still hold closely to Him. His gentle voice—soft as the breath of even—can whisper words of guidance and strength. We, too, can come boldly (παρρησία: *parrhēsia*—literally, 'telling everything') unto the throne of grace (He 4₁₆).

It is well worth while giving careful observation to the **double compounds** of Paul. When he writes: 'The Spirit also helpeth our infirmity', he uses a **verb** (συναντιλαμβάνεται: *sunantilambanetai*) which was widely employed throughout the whole of the Hellenistic world (Rom. 8₂₆). It literally means 'take hold along with'. If we have to push something heavy, it makes a tremendous difference when some stronger person comes to our aid. The Holy Spirit, whose glory is extolled in the eighth chapter of the Epistle to the Romans, is said by Paul to come to our very side to support us in our weakness. Especially is this so in the matter of intercession, for our prayers are so often ineffective.

The preacher can find many luminous suggestions in **Greek superlatives**. Paul seems to revel in words like ὑπερβάλλω (*huperballo*), ὑπερπλεονάζω (*huperpleonazō*), ὑπερυψόω (*huperupso-ō*), ὑπεραυξάνω (*huperauxanō*). The vast resources of a Pagan Empire or the widespread ramifications of evil never depressed him who was convinced that God highly exalted (ὑπερύψωσεν: *huperupsosen*) Jesus. (The **aorist** shows that the reference is to the historical fact of the Ascension.) It is the Father's gracious favour (ἐχαρίσατο: *echarisato*) to make the crucified Redeemer the enthroned Lord, before whose majesty all creation should bow (Ph 2₉₋₁₀). Does not the preacher today often lose the thrill of visualizing the majestic Christ, the Superman? Christ receives the worship which belongs to the Eternal. If God is on our side, what does it matter who is against us?

It is interesting to pursue Paul's use of the **preposition** σύν (*sun*). Someone has calculated that he mentions sixty of his friends in his letters and that Luke refers to twenty-five. Though the number mentioned in the Acts hardly amounts to so many, yet it is very evident that the apostle had numerous friends. Some are very delightfully described as 'beloved', e.g., Rom 1⁷ 1 Co 4₁₄ Ph 2₁₂ (ἀγαπητός: *agapētos*), whilst others are revealed as intimate workers with him in Christian service. The many συν-compounds open up a useful line of thought.

For instance, a happy analogy can be recognized between the relationship of Paul's friends to the apostle and that of Paul to his Lord.   In each case God is seen at work.

(1)   There is A COMMON CAUSE *to be served*.   A friend is termed a συστρατιώτης (*sustratiōtēs*) or a σύνδουλος (*sundoulos*). Paul speaks of some Philippian women in Ph 4₃—συνήθλησαν μοι μετά (*sunethlēsan moi meta*)—as if they strenuously exerted themselves along with him in a great athletic contest.   Similarly, Paul considers that he is linked with Christ in a glorious Cause: 'We beseech you (Ὑπὲρ Χριστοῦ πρεσβεύομεν: *huper Christou presbeuomen*) on behalf of Christ' (2 Co 5₂₀).   Εἴπερ συνπάσχομεν ἵνα καὶ συνδοξασθῶμεν (*eiper sunpaschomen hina kai sundoxasthōmen*)—'If so be that we suffer with Him, that we may be also glorified with Him' (Ro 8₁₇).

(2)   In each case SACRIFICE IS TRANSFORMED BY FRIENDSHIP. Though medical men could command high fees in apostolic times, Luke ('the beloved physician') kept by the side of Paul in Philippi, accompanied him to Jerusalem, watched over him in his imprisonment, sailed with him to Rome, and proved a loyal friend to the last.   It took no small courage for Onesimus to return to Colossae and for Philemon to forgive his dishonest slave.   But Paul had a wonderful way with him.   It was a dim reflection of the manner in which Christ was able to make the apostle gladly suffer the loss of all things.   The love of Christ 'constrained' (2 Co 5₁₄) him (συνέχω: *sunechō*) is used in Luke 22₆₃ of 'keeping a firm hold of' Jesus when He was arrested.

> *Love took up the harp of life, and smote on all the chords with might;*
> *Smote the chord of self, that, trembling, pass'd in music out of sight.*

When Paul spoke of 'gaining' Christ, (Ph 3₈) he used a **verb** (κερδαίνω: *kerdainō*) which is found in Ja 4₁₃ with the meaning 'to gain a profit in a commercial transaction'.   His friendship with the Risen Lord transformed every sacrifice into a privilege.

(3)   Once more, the analogy holds good in regard to

IMMORTAL INFLUENCE. When Paul chose Phoebe to convey the
Epistle to the Romans, and when Epaphroditus risked his life
for the apostle, they did not dream of the immeasurable value
of their service. Their names and work are imperishably
preserved. Similarly, the aged prisoner did not conceive that
the letters which he wrote in his cell and the sacrificial service
which he counted a joy to render would prove the means by
which his living Lord would become a priceless treasure to
people of succeeding generations and of all lands.

Sometimes the *use of a particular Greek word* will enable a
preacher to illustrate a familiar fact from a fresh point of view.
In Ac 8₄ we read: 'They therefore that were scattered abroad
(διασπαρέντες: *diasparentes*) went about preaching the word.'
We know that διασπείρω (*diaspeirō*) is the usual word for
'sowing' seed. The **verb** has a peculiar aptness in this passage, for a glorious harvest was afterwards to be reaped, inasmuch as the persecution of the Christians led to a widespread
sowing of the seed of the Divine Word.

The use of a **singular** or **plural** is worthy of attention.
'Simon, Simon,' said our Lord, 'behold Satan obtained you
(ὑμᾶς: *humas*) by asking that he might sift you as wheat; but I
made supplication for thee (σοῦ: *sou*) that thy faith fail not'
(Lk 22₃₁). We observe here the personal concern which Jesus
had for Peter. Moreover, if the **aorist** ἐξητήσατο (*exetesato*)
suggests that Satan succeeded in his petition, equally does the
aorist ἐδεήθην (*edeēthen*) imply that at the same time Jesus
interceded for His wayward and impulsive disciple.

The importance of noting the *variation of tenses* is well illustrated in Ro 6₁₃, though neither the AV nor the RV discloses
the difference. As the **present active imperative** of παρ-
ιστάνω (*paristanō*) is used here we might translate the original:
'Do not go on presenting your members unto sin. . . .' This is
followed by a call to dedication in one decisive act, because
the **verb** παρ-ίστημι is now in the **1st aorist active
imperative**: 'But present yourselves to God.' This gives
the preacher an opportunity of making an appeal for instant
decision.

When a **verb** is in the **middle voice** there is implied a sense
of responsibility resting upon those who hear the message, as

in 2 P 1₁₀, where it is meant that the readers of the Epistle are
to make an effort themselves: 'Give the more diligence to make
(ποιεῖσθαι: poieisthai) your calling and election sure.' Again,
in He 1₃ we read: 'When He had made (ποιησάμενος: poiesa-
menos) purification of sins.' The **middle voice** suggests that
Christ Himself in His own Person (and not by something dis-
tinct from Himself) made the purification.

The Greek language is full of little graphic and delicate
shades of meaning. Take, for example, Mk 5₂₈, where ἔλεγεν
(elegen) is translated: 'She said.' As this **verb** is in the **im-
perfect tense,** it is implied that the unfortunate woman kept
on repeating to herself: 'If I touch but His garments, I shall
be made whole.' How wonderfully did she realize (what
psychologists are emphasizing today) the value of repeating
over and over again some positive affirmation like: 'I can do
all things in Him that strengtheneth me' (Ph 4₁₃). We can
appreciate the value of suggestion in our prayers of thanksgiving. This, indeed, was a characteristic of the prayers of the
early Christians.

Ignatius described a public service as 'a meeting for thanksgiving'. Origen advised his fellow Christians to open their
public worship with thanksgiving. And even when a Christian was detained in a prison and his plans upset for preaching
the Gospel to every creature, he wrote to his friends at Philippi
and said: 'Rejoice in the Lord alway. . . . In everything by
prayer and supplication with thanksgiving (μετὰ εὐχαριστίας:
meta eucharistias) let your requests be made known unto God'
(Ph 4₆₋₆). This word was frequently used in the papyri for
'gratitude' after a real benefactor had helped a friend.

The observance of the **present tense** of ἔρχομαι (erchomai)
in Jn 14₁₈ reminds us that the AV is incorrect in translating: 'I
will not leave you comfortless, I will come to you.' Our Lord
is coming now to every heart that welcomes Him. Again, if
the preacher is expounding Jn 15₁₆ he will notice that three
present active subjunctives are used with ἵνα (hina) to
emphasize the continued realization of the purpose of Christ.
As heralds of the Gospel and as those who would seek to ensure
the perpetuity of the Church, Christ's disciples must KEEP ON
GOING (ὑπάγητε : hupagēte), KEEP ON BEARING (φέρητε: pherēte)

fruit, KEEP ON PRODUCING SUCH FRUIT AS WOULD REMAIN (μένῃ: *mene*).

The preacher stands in the pulpit as the representative of the living God. Some of his congregation need comfort, some require guidance and yet others have not enjoyed an inward experience of the love of Christ. How it strengthens the gracious promise in Jn 6₃₇ to observe the **strong double negation**: οὐ μὴ ἐκβάλω ἔξω (*ou me ekbalō exō*). Though Jesus said that He would 'cast out' (the same Greek word) the Prince of this world (Jn 12₃₁), yet He would not under any circumstance whatsoever 'cast out' the person who came in penitence and faith to Him.

Similarly, the tenderness and beauty of another promise is enhanced as we examine the Greek in He 13₅, where there are no less than five **negatives**. We might paraphrase the sentence: 'Never, never, never, never, under no circumstances—be they ever so difficult—will I desert you.' The Greek here has something more with which to comfort us. Ἀνίημι (*aniĕmi*) is used elsewhere about the loosing of prisoners' chains (Ac 16₂₆); and ἐγκαταλείπω (*egkataleipō*) is found in Mt 27₄₆ about our Lord's cry of dereliction on the Cross. In this great promise we have ground for the most confident faith. 'I will never, never loosen My hold of you nor leave you forsaken in an utterly helpless condition.'

A sermon becomes all the more interesting when **abstract** terms are avoided and **picturesque words** used. Jesus set us an excellent example in this respect in the way He clothed His truths with pictures from nature and from life. His parables were illuminating and His miracles were signs (σημεῖα: *semeia*). Many passages of the Greek Testament unfold lovely and surprising pictures. Ἀναζωπυρέω (*anazōpureo*) in 2 Ti 1₆ is a case in point. Paul exhorts Timothy to 'stir up the gift of God'. The verb literally means to rekindle or keep blazing. John Wesley makes this comment: 'Literally, blowing up the coals into a flame' (*Notes on the New Testament*). We will recall how his brother worked out the theme in one of his greatest hymns:

> Still let me guard the holy fire,
> And still stir up Thy gift in me.

Again, Paul says: 'Walk worthily of the calling (κλῆσις: *klesis*) wherewith ye were called' (Eph 4₁). This Greek word, which is translated 'vocation' in the New Testament, had interesting associations in early times: (i) a command to attend the king's court, (ii) an invitation to a feast, (iii) a summons to appear as a witness in a law-court. We can see how readily these points can constitute an interesting sermon. As Christians we must be worthily dressed with the garments of love and lowliness, we must be joyous and ready to bear our witness to Christ's saving and keeping power.

The **colour of a Greek word** in one place may help to interpret and illuminate another passage. Take our Lord's call, as recorded in Mk 8₃₄: 'If any man would come after me, let him deny himself. . . .' 'Ἀπαρνέομαι (*aparneomai*), which is translated 'deny' here, is an **intensive** form of the **verb**. It is used in our Lord's reference to Peter: 'Before the cock crow twice, thou shalt deny (ἀπαρνήσῃ: *aparnēsē*) me thrice' (Mk 14₃₀). Now the meaning of that denial is crystallized in the phrase: 'I know not the man.' It follows, therefore, that whosoever would follow Christ must be willing to say to the self that seeks flattery, indulgence, and priority: 'I know not the man.' When self is ignored and Christ becomes all in all, there is a new creation. Nothing but the transforming friendship of Christ can accomplish that change.

Finally, many original and profitable sermons can be made out of Greek words whose meaning has been lit up by our *knowledge of the papyri*. Wordsworth, longing for the recovery of the works of an early writer, said (in his poem, 'Upon the same occasion') :

> *O ye, who patiently explore*
> *The wreck of Herculanean lore,*
> *What rapture! could ye seize*
> *Some Theban fragment, or unroll*
> *One precious, tender-hearted, scroll*
> *Of pure Simonides.*

The young preacher who ploughs his way through the vocabulary of the Greek New Testament and reads the books unfolding the latest archaeological discoveries will find treasure

untold.   Deissmann said that the number of words peculiar
to the New Testament is about fifty or one per cent.   The
papyri reveal that the language of the New Testament is the
language of the vernacular Greek, and not the language of
contemporary literature.   The Gospels and Epistles were
written for the common people.   'The key to the under-
standing of the New Testament Documents', says H. G. G.
Herklots (*A Fresh Approach to the New Testament*), 'is that they
are the propagandist literature of a widespread and successful
missionary movement.'   Even the polished language of Luke,
who was termed by Jerome 'the most erudite of the Evangelists', is strikingly different from the artificial Greek of contemporary rhetorical authors.

Many a text will be enriched by illustrations from the
papyri. $Λογίζομαι$ (*logizomai*), for instance, is a metaphor
from accountancy ('take account of') and has three interesting
applications in Ph 4_8, 1 Co 13_5 and Ro 8_{18}.   We shall notice
further illustrations later in this book.   It should be said, too,
that it is important to observe how the language of the New
Testament is used in the Greek version of the Old Testament—
the Septuagint.   For instance, $ἱλάσκομαι$ (*hilaskomai*) means
in classical Greek and in the *Koine* 'to propitiate or placate' a
deity, whereas in the LXX it signifies 'to expiate' or be a means
of delivering man from sin.

To those who prayerfully and thoughtfully study their
Greek Testament there is unlocked 'the golden casket where
gems of truth are stored'.   In the light of the Holy Spirit these
gems scintillate with a rare beauty and a divine brilliance.

PART TWO

The Exposition of the Word of God

One

'WHAT MANNER OF LOVE'
(1 John 3₁)

'BEHOLD what manner of (ποταπὴν: *potapēn*) love the Father hath bestowed upon us,' says John, 'that we should be called children (τέκνα: *tekna*) of God' (1 Jn 3₁). Ποταπός (*potapos*) meant in classical literature: 'Of what country?' The picture behind the word is that of an inhabitant of a seaport who, on beholding the arrival of some distinguished-looking person, exclaims: 'From what country does he come?' (Note the use of this Greek adjective also in Mt 8₂₇ and 2 P 3₁₁.) The more the aged John meditated on the love of God, the more he was filled with wonder at the uniqueness of it. There is something unearthly about the divine love. The New Testament writers cannot help using a distinctive word (ἀγάπη: *agapē*) to indicate its rare quality. Human love is so often kindled by the love of a friend; but divine love is utterly and absolutely unselfish.

Pointing out the supernatural nature of God's love, Dr Herbert H. Farmer says in his book *God and Man* that there are three reasons why this distinctive quality of divine love should be made clear. 'First, because it is only as men can be brought to see the divine love in this its undiscriminating absoluteness and universality that they can be convinced of its reality. Its unmotivated universality, requiring no attractive qualities in a person to call it forth, does not make it unbelievable; rather, it is that which makes it believable—as an attribute of God. Second, without some vision of the divine love as agape, no man can even begin to have a deep, sincere, and poignant awareness of his own sinful lovelessness and of the need for, as well as the wonder of, God's forgiveness.   Third, only by emphasizing the essential non-dependence of God's love upon the qualities of the person loved can we dispose of the notion that the Christian doctrine of God as love really ascribes to Him a weak and sentimental unrealism.'   On the Cross, which can draw all men to God, we see divine love shining forth in all the splendour of its unselfishness.

A fragment from an early manuscript is restored in the Revised Version in 1 Jn 3₂: 'And such we are.'   That we are children of God is no empty title.   The word for 'children' (τέκνα: *tekna*) in the passage which we are considering is found in the papyri as a term of endearment and was applied to grown-up people.   This intensifies the sense of God's love to us.

An old philosopher once said: 'If Caesar should adopt you, no one could endure your pride.'   But it seems to be inferred in John's first Epistle that love, not pride, will be the characteristic of the children of God.   Just as sons and daughters reveal striking resemblances to their parents and express many of their qualities of character, so with those who are born of God.   'If we love one another, God abideth in us, and His love is perfected in us' (1Jn 4₁₂).   We are made partakers (κοινωνοί: *koinōnoi*) of the divine nature (2 P 1₄).   If even a dew-drop can sparkle with the glory of the sun, the humblest believer can reflect the divine love.

Two

'THE LORD IS MY HELPER'
(Hebrews 13₆)

It was when Christians 'endured a great conflict of sufferings' that the author of the Epistle to the Hebrews wrote: 'With good courage we say, The Lord is my helper (βοηθός: *boēthos*); I will not fear: what shall man do unto me?' (He 13₆).

There are four picturesque Greek words which are translated 'help'.   They are full of suggestion for those who believe (like the poet Tennyson) that prayer opens the sluice gates between God and the human soul. The divine power comes pouring into our impotent lives, clearing our minds, refreshing our sluggish sympathies and speeding our will in abounding service.

(1) Βοηθέω (boētheō)—which is related to the word in He 13₆ —is an old **compound verb** (bōe, a cry; thein, to run). It suggests *running to the cry of one who calls for help*. It is found in the story of the Canaanitish woman, who in her desperate anxiety about her sick daughter came to Jesus saying: 'Lord, help me' (Mt 15₂₅). The same word is found in connexion with Paul's vision of the man of Macedonia who besought him saying: 'Come over into Macedonia and help (boētheson) us' (Acts 16₉). Though Greece was the home of art, poetry and philosophy, and though Rome glorified in its powerful armies, its magnificent palaces, its great laws, and its far-flung imperial interests, there was a moral impotence in those civilizations which nothing but the Gospel of Christ could heal.

Civilization is the modern 'Man of Macedonia' crying to the Christian Church: 'Come over and help us.' All material schemes of improvement may seem attractive and even delightful; but like flowers on a grave, they do not in themselves put an end to the corruption beneath.

(2) A second word which is translated 'help' (συναντι-λαμβάνομαι: sunantilambanomai) literally means '*lay hold along with*'. It is used in the **middle voice** in regard to Martha's request to Jesus that He should bid her give a helping hand (Lk 10₄₀). The word is also employed about the Holy Spirit helping us in our infirmities (Ro 8₂₆). This applies especially to the matter of prayer. There is often the temptation to let our minds wander.

> *My words fly up, my thoughts remain below.*
> *Words without thought never to heaven go.*

There is also much ignorance in our praying. We ask for the wrong things or we lack passion in our intercession. As the Holy Spirit comes to make our hearts His home, His sacred voice speaks in us and for us to the gracious Hearer of prayer. We are thereby delivered from absorption in trivial interests;

matters of surpassing importance come to our minds. The depth of inbred sin is revealed and the welcome relief of the Father's mercy becomes a haven of refuge.

The Holy Spirit clothes our words with a power of persuasiveness which language cannot express. 'He maketh intercession for us with groanings which cannot be uttered.' We are immensely helped.

(3)   The third Greek word translated 'help' (ἐπικουρία: *epikouria*) is used in Homer with the sense of *acting as an ally*. In modern times the value of an ally intensifies the sense of security. Many a small nation has been saved from disturbing fears because of the assurance that all the rich resources of a mighty nation would be available in any case of emergency. In every emergency the apostle Paul had an Ally. (See the use of ἐπικουριά (*epikouria*) in Ac 26₂₂.)

(4)   The fourth word for 'help' (συνυπουργέω: *sunupourgeo*) reminds us of the assistance which we ourselves can give to others through prayer. The Greek term means 'to serve' or *work together*. Though there are other words which suggest co-operation, *sunupourgeo* is worthy of notice, because in the only place where it is used in the New Testament the reference is to prayer (2 Co 1₁₁). Paul reminds his friends that he is dependent on their co-operation in prayer when further perils confront him.

Συνυπουργέω (*sunupourgeō*) has the Greek word for 'work' (ἔργον: *ergon*) enshrined in it. The suggestion of strenuous wrestling in intercession is in Paul's mind when he speaks of others striving together with him in prayer.

Three

'FOLLOW ME'
(Luke 5₂₇)

Ἀκολουθέω (*akoloutheō*) occurs nearly eighty times in the New Testament. Before we observe the richness of this term we must take note of the Authorized Reading in Mt 4₁₉: 'Follow me; and I will make you fishers of men.' The first phrase in this sentence is more correctly rendered in the Revised Version. 'Come ye after me' (Δεῦτε ὀπίσω μου: *deute opisō mou*). This is a call to obedience. 'I will make (ποιήσω: *poiēsō*) you.' This **verb** was used in connexion with apprenticeship in certain arts and crafts. Those who 'come after' Christ learn the art of catching men. Carlyle used to advise others to 'study some earnest, deep-minded, truth-loving man, to work their way into his manner of thought, till they could see with his eyes, feel as he felt and judge as he judged, neither believing nor denying till they could in some measure so feel and judge.' Similarly, Jesus called His disciples to learn of Him.

Two of the three Greek terms for 'net' are of special interest here. Travellers in Palestine inform us that they have seen the ἀμφίβληστρον (*amphiblēstron*) used. This pear-shaped net was thrown by hand from the shore or from a fishing-boat. As it was skilfully wielded, the net opened out and the edges being weighted sank immediately to the bottom: thus the fish within the area were caught. There is only one place in the whole lake (and that near Bethsaida) where fishermen can wade into the water a reasonable distance without getting out of their depth; and it was probably there that Jesus called Peter and Andrew (Mt 4₁₈). The δίκτυον (*diktuon*) was a larger form of net. It was lowered from a boat in night-fishing. It is found in the story of the great draught of fishes (Jn 21 ₆, ₈, ₁₁).

As fish are repelled by stale nets, the winner of souls must ever keep near the Source of cleansing and victorious living. It is interesting to note that the very Greek word which is used for the 'mending' of torn nets in Mk 1₁₉ is used by Peter regarding the 'perfecting' of Church members (1 P 5₁₀). In a world full of difficulties, discouragements, and sin, the grace of patience is an indispensable qualification of a Christian disciple. J. R. Lowell's words regarding Columbus have a wider application:

> *The inspired soul but flings his patience in,*
> *And slowly that outweighs the ponderous globe—*
> *One faith against a whole world's unbelief,*
> *One soul against the flesh of all mankind.*

When our Lord called His disciples to be 'fishers of men'
He asked them first to 'follow' (ἀκολουθεῖν: *akolouthein*) Him
(Lk 5₂₇). 'Following' Christ implies something deeper than
'coming after Him'. '*Akoloutheo*' is used in the papyri about
someone who is advised to stick to another and so become his
friend. Christ delights to see acquaintanceship developing
into friendship and friendship deepening into loyalty. This
relationship necessarily inspires a sense of power; and in the
craft of winning souls power is indispensable. Many a poor
Pagan longed for a better life. The prayer of Cleanthes was
praiseworthy:

> *Lead Thou me on, O Zeus and Destiny,*
> *To that goal long ago to me assigned.*
> *I'll follow and not falter; if my will*
> *Prove weak and craven, I will follow still.*

But many a man finds that the human will has its limitations.
The good that he would do, he does not. But, when a man
lives in the climate of Christ's friendship, duty gives way to joy,
weariness to power, and failure to success.

Thus, having lived in fellowship with his Divine Master, the
Christian fisherman will have (i) *Vision*—As the sea is full of
fish, so there are many unbelievers; (ii) *Skill*—The best conditions, the most suitable appeal and the most appropriate time
will be considered; (iii) *Patience*—An indispensable requisite;
(iv) *Self-suppression*—Above all other things, self must be kept
in the background. Izaak Walton in his *Compleat Angler*
points out that in the art of angling, experience is more important than studying books. 'I will make you,' says the
Master. Live with Me, and you will be equipped. What
thrilling joys await those who are guided to win souls!

Four

'THE FULNESS OF CHRIST'
(Ephesians 1₂₃)

THE word πλήρωμα (*plēroma*) fills a large place in literature.   It
was used for 'the full strength' of a naval vessel, a military unit,
and the 'totality' of the divine powers and attributes; and yet,
again, it signified the total of many sums of money.   Professor
C. H. Dodd says (in the *Abingdon Commentary*): 'What concerns
us here is the fact that it was used by both Christian and non-
Christian Gnostics as a technical term for the totality of
"powers", "emanations", "aeons", or whatever term was used
for superhuman orders of beings supposed to intervene between
man and the Absolute.   Paul takes over from the Colossian
"heretics" their quasi-philosophical term—not precisely in the
same sense, since his philosophy was not theirs, but in a sense
which they would understand.   For him it means the sum of
the divine attributes and powers, not as distributed through a
hierarchy of spiritual beings, but as concentrated in the one
God.'

It seems that in his prison Epistles Paul has in mind the
amazing thought that as God dwelt in Christ in all His
totality, Christ would dwell in the Church.   'The Church,
which is His body, the fulness (πλήρωμα: *plērōma*) of Him that
filleth all in all' (Eph 1₂₃).   When the Apostle speaks of
Church members 'attaining unto the unity of the faith and of
the knowledge of the Son of God, unto a full-grown man, unto
the measure of the stature of the fulness of Christ', he is thinking
of the collective aspect of the Church.   If the Church is to be
the medium through which Christ is to reconcile all the con-
flicting interests and divisions of the world, it necessarily follows that the Church must have all its own divisions healed.
It must express Christ in His totality.

It should be observed that a significant **verb** is used in
Col 1₁₉: 'In Him (i.e. Christ) should all the fulness dwell'
(κατοικῆσαι: *katoikēsai*).   Heretical teachers conceived only
of a partial and transient connexion of the *pleroma* with the

Lord. Paul uses a **strong verb** which means a permanent abode. The full character of God and the complete content of the Divine attributes dwelt permanently in Christ. So, likewise, Paul prays that Christ may make His settled abode in believers' hearts (Eph 3₁₇). This wonderful vision of the majesty and intimacy of Christ is truly enheartening. All the pools of our need and sin are covered over and cleansed by the incoming tide of God's grace. Behind that tide there are unimaginable resources.

Five

'THAT THEY SHOULD KNOW THEE, THE ONLY TRUE GOD'
(John 17₃)

THE **verb** γινώσκω (*ginoskō*), which occurs nearly one hundred and ninety times in the New Testament, frequently indicates an intimate relationship. It is more than an intellectual apprehension. There is involved a mystical experience and the word often implies that what is known is of value to the person who knows it. It may also carry with it the idea of approval on the part of God. In a familiar passage, Paul says: 'Howbeit the firm foundation of God standeth, having this seal, The Lord knoweth (ἔγνω: *egnō*) them that are His' (2 Ti 2₁₉). It seems as if the same thought underlies the intimate relationship suggested in Jn 10₂₇: 'My sheep hear my voice, and I know (γινώσκω: *ginosko*) them and they follow me.' Similarly in Gal 4₉.

Generally speaking, '*ginosko*' is to be differentiated from οἶδα (*oida*) in that the former suggests inception or progress in knowledge whilst *oida* implies fulness of knowledge. For instance, our Lord said to the Jews: 'Ye have not known (ἐγνώκατε: *egnōkate*) him: but I know (οἶδα: *oida*) him' (Jn 8₅₅). There is the idea of perception behind οἶδα (*oida*). We read in a papyrus: 'See that you do not detain him, for you know οἶδας (*oidas*) how I have need of him every hour.' Similarly,

Peter did not understand our Lord's gracious act in washing the disciples' feet, so his Master said: 'What I do thou knowest (οἶδας: *oidas*) not now; but thou shalt understand (γνώσῃ: *gnōse*) hereafter' (Jn 13₇). Peter's insight into the significance of that impressive sacramental act would develop till one day he would grasp its great meaning. Nobody has fully realized the love of Christ. It resembles as it were a lofty mountain that has to be explored. Paul tried to outline its dimensions, but he was compelled to admit that it defied all measurement. Yet he prays for his friends that they may be able to know (γνῶναι: *gnōnai*) it. He knew that when they cultivated the spirit of fellowship ('with all the saints') they would make fresh discoveries in their exploration of a mighty experience. Intellectual knowledge was unduly exalted in the Churches where Greeks predominated. But it had to be pointed out by those who were Christian leaders that such knowledge had to be linked with spiritual perception and ethical living. 'We know (οἶδαμεν: *oidamen*)'—that is through intuition—'that we have passed out of death into life, because we love the brethren' (1 Jn 3₁₄). Farther on the same writer adds the words: 'Hereby know we (ἐγνώκαμεν: *egnōkamen*) love.' This knowledge arises from the progressive experience of the Divine teaching. (Compare 1 Jn 3₁₆.)

It is instructive to note that γινώσκω (*ginōskō*) is found in Jn 17₃: 'This is life eternal, that (*hina*) they should know (γινώσκωσιν: *ginōskōsin*) thee the only true God, and him whom thou didst send, even Jesus Christ.' This **present active subjunctive tense** involves a continuing idea of intimacy. Ἵνα (*hina*: 'that') implies that there is an aim; and until that aim is realized there must be a constant development in knowledge. As we have indicated above, this knowledge is not merely an intellectual apprehension of external facts; it involves an appropriating faith—a personal laying hold of Christ. This is no sentimental mysticism but a means whereby the rich quality of the divine love can flow forth as a healing stream to mankind.

Our Lord Himself claimed the unique distinction of communicating the knowledge of God His Father (Mt 11₂₅₋₂₇). It carried with it a challenge to live in the spirit of love as becometh

2

children of God. This knowledge brings with it the most precious of all gifts—the gift of eternal life ($\zeta\omega\acute{\eta}$: $z\bar{o}\bar{e}$). This Greek word is to be distinguished from $\beta\acute{\iota}os$ ($bios$) which in the papyri is used to connote 'duration of life', 'livelihood', and 'manner of life'. When Paul writes, 'No soldier on service entangleth himself in the affairs of this life' (2 Ti 2₄), it is $\beta\acute{\iota}os$ ($bios$) he uses. $Z\omega\acute{\eta}$ ($z\bar{o}\bar{e}$), on the other hand, signifies the highest blessedness; it is the quality of life that exists in God. The familiar biblical expressions such as 'the tree of life' (Rev 2₇), 'the crown of life' (Rev 2₁₀), 'the life of God' (Eph 4₁₈), and 'the power of an endless life' (He 7₁₆)—all contain this opulent word.

Jesus accepted much of the Old Testament teaching about life. In the many noble passages which nourished His soul, the Father is conceived of as 'the living God', full of peace and power, righteousness and love. This life can be appropriated by the believer. We recall how our Lord quoted Dt 8₃: 'Man doth not live by bread only, but by everything that proceedeth out of the mouth of the Lord'. Since life is the very essence of the Divine Being, it can only become the believer's experience through communion with God. 'With Thee is the fountain of life' (Psalm 36₉).

In one sense it may be said that life is set forth in the New Testament as a future reward (Mt 7₁₄). The Book of Revelation is full of the idea. Yet we cannot overlook the fact that our Lord believed that His friends could enjoy a present blessedness or life. The Prodigal Son who had come home 'was dead and is alive again'. It would be true to say that the future blessedness of the believer is really a heightening of the same kind of experience realized when the believer enjoys close fellowship with God.

Paul uses $\grave{\epsilon}\pi\acute{\iota}\gamma\nu\omega\sigma\iota s$ ($epign\bar{o}sis$) in many of his references to God (Eph 4₁₃). The forcefulness of the **prefix** rivets attention on the object of knowledge. On the whole, the papyri hardly support the popular interpretation that $epignosis$ implies fuller and more complete knowledge. In He 10₂₆ we are again reminded by the use of $\lambda\alpha\mu\beta\acute{\alpha}\nu\omega$ ($lamban\bar{o}$) that knowledge of the truth is a divine gift.

Six

'JESUS CHRIST WAS OPENLY SET FORTH CRUCIFIED'

(Galatians 3₁)

WE CAN appreciate the keen sense of disappointment which Paul felt when he wrote these pathetic words: 'O foolish Galatians, who did bewitch (ἐβάσκανεν: *ebaskanen*) you, before whose very eyes Jesus Christ was openly set forth crucified (προεγράφη: *proegraphē*)?' (Gal 3₁). The Greek word βασκαίνω (*baskainō*) means to lead astray by the power of the evil eye. It is found in an ancient papyrus document which reads: 'Above all, we pray that you may be in health, unharmed by the evil eye, and faring sumptuously.' The apostle could not understand how the Galatians relapsed into Jewish legalism, especially as the Jews had the crucified 'openly set forth' (προγράφω: *prographō*) before their very eyes. This Greek **verb** was used in early times by fathers who posted up proclamations about their sons' debts. Paul had set forth the Cross, not in cold abstract terms but in appealing pictures. If the apostle were in the flesh today he would say: 'I made the Cross as realistic as a cinema film.' There was the sad procession to Calvary, the mocking scorn, the crown of thorns, the hammering of nails into the hands that had offered healing to the most unworthy and into the feet that had walked on many an errand of love. Even though there was the jeering of the crowds, the gambling of the soldiers and the apathy of the multitude, nothing but words of love and forgiveness came from the lips of Him Whose body was racked with pain and Whose heart was broken with the burden of sin. Paul marvelled that such a wondrous scene had not made a more lasting impression on the Galatians. Why did they allow themselves to be so foolishly drawn away?

We can see from this verse (Gal 3₁) three things: (i) The IMPRESSION which the Cross obviously made on Paul. He determined to know nothing but Christ and Him crucified (1 Co 2₂); (ii) the EXPRESSION of the Cross. Paul related it to

the home (Eph 5₂₅), society (Ro 14₁₅) and the world (Col 1₂₀);
(iii) the SUPPPRESSION of the Cross by the Galatians. They
were bewitched. They allowed the Cross to be largely sub-
merged by non-essentials and thus were open to the danger of
rejecting it altogether.

Seven

'THE FELLOWSHIP OF THE HOLY SPIRIT'
(2 Corinthians 13₁₄)

THE Church was created into a fellowship of the Holy Spirit
at Pentecost. Luke informs us that the spiritually-endowed
Church after that memorable occasion 'continued stedfastly
in the apostles' teaching and in "the" fellowship, in the breaking of bread and the prayers' (Ac 2₄₂). This sense of 'to-
getherness' was a very wonderful fact. There are several
characteristics of this 'fellowship' (κοινωνία: koinōnia) worthy
of notice.

(1) It is a *divine fellowship*. The Church is far more than
a club or a mutual help association. It is a divine fellowship.
It exists by sharing the life of Christ. It comprises the people
of God, an ideal Israel, a God-created community. *Koinōnia*
had many interesting and suggestive associations. It was used
in the papyri for the closest of all human relationships—marriage. It is to be differentiated from μετέχω (*metechō*) (which
means to partake of) in that it implies active participation; and
the effect of such fellowship depends on the co-operation of the
recipient as well as on the attitude of the giver. For instance,
we read in 1 Co 10₁₆ (RV marginal reading): 'The cup of
blessing which we bless, is it not a participation (κοινωνία:
koinōnia) of the blood of Christ? The bread which we break,
is it not a participation (κοινωνία: *koinōnia*) of the body of
Christ?' The single loaf, broken, distributed and eaten,
united the many members who partook of it; the life of Christ
dwelt in them; and they formed a community in close fellowship with their Redeemer.

Κοινωνός (*koinōnos*) is used in Lk 5₁₀ in reference to James and John who were 'partners' with Simon in owning a little fishing fleet. Greek writers illustrate this use of the word. Paul speaks of his friends in Philippi as being joint-shareholders (*συνκοινωνοί*: *sunkoinōnoi*) with him in grace. As Prof. C. H. Dodd points out (*The Moffatt Commentary on* 1 *John*), Christians hold shares together in the Gospel (1 Co 9₂₃), in faith (Philem 6), in sufferings (Ph 3₁₀), in comfort (2 Co 1₇), in the Holy Spirit (2 Co 13₁₄) and in future glory (1 P 5₁). This rich quality of common life and this wonderful and continual inter-flow of the power of the Holy Spirit into the lives of the early Christians brought about a stupendous achievement—the formation of an *ekklēsia* that could not only withstand the bitterest onslaughts of its enemies but resulted in the collapse of the towering institutions of the Pagan world. The Church was a God-created fellowship.

(2) The Church is *a purposeful fellowship.* If the members suffered with one another and shared the common life drawn from Christ through the Holy Spirit, it was to express it in service and manifest it in work. A fellowship can only function efficiently when there is a common (*κοινός*: *koinos*) purpose actuating it. Though we must ever bear in mind that the dominant sense of *koinōnia* is the inner experience—the sharing of the gift of the Spirit—yet we cannot but fail to see that this fellowship involved outward expression. This was seen in (*a*) *Public Prayers*; (*b*) the *mutual supply of material goods.* 'All they that believed together held all things common' (*κοινά*: *koina*) (Ac 2₄₄); (*c*) the *Collection for the saints.* This contribution of money is called *koinonia* in 2 Co 9₁₃, because Paul regarded it as the emblem and instrument of the corporate fellowship which knit together the locally scattered Christian Church. The word *koinōnia* was used in the papyri for financial contributions such as 'for the rent'; and no doubt Paul received financial help from his friends when he was imprisoned in Philippi. He valued it as a symbol of that deep sympathy which through the power of the Holy Spirit made Christian love an exceedingly precious thing (Ph 1₅, 4₁₄₋₁₅); (*d*) Christians share also in PRACTICAL SERVICE—even in the SERVICE OF OTHERS. They might share the joy of a spiritual

harvest, of which they had not sowed the seed (Jn 4₃₆₋₃₈).
Like the many branches of the one vine there was a unity made
possible by a sharing in the same life of the one tree. Every
true member could gladly claim that his fellowship (*koinonia*)
was with the Father and with His Son Jesus Christ (1 Jn 1₃).
And that blest communion extends into the unseen. The
writer of the Epistle to the Hebrews speaks of a blessed fellowship with innumerable hosts of angels in festive gathering, the
assembly of the firstborn whose names are enrolled as citizens
in the heavenly city (He 12 ₂₂₋₂₃).

But *koinonia* implies not only a God-made fellowship, a God-
directed fellowship, but also:

(3) A *God-uniting fellowship*. The community of believers
in the first century was a marvellous and miraculous creation.
Though famous Stoic philosophers had said noble things about
the brotherhood of man, yet there was nothing approaching
the fellowship of the Christian Church, which united people
of the most diverse conditions. The bigoted Jew was loved
by the proud Roman and the cultured Greek. The Jew was
even willing to transfer the sacred name of Israel to the Gentile,
who used to be considered worse than the despised dog of the
street. The aristocrat and the slave could meet together in a
little church-house and tell of what their Saviour had done for
them. This great brotherhood was world-wide (1 P 5₉).
And the high ethical standards which these little colonies of
Christians attained led to the development and growth of the
Church.

It is quite true that sometimes in the early Church (as in
Corinth, for instance) the members fell into sin. Strife,
jealousy, wrath, factions, backbitings, whisperings, and other
sins caused division. But Paul's remedy for such unworthy
conduct was the doctrine of the one Body. To the Philippians
he said: 'If there is any fellowship (κοινωνία: *koinōnia*) of the
Spirit. . . . be of the same mind, having the same love, being
of one accord (σύμψυχοι: *sumpsuchoi*), of one mind' (Ph 2₁₋₂).
The Greek word just quoted literally means 'sharing the same
soul'. The Church must have no divisions; it must be one
organism, one body, sharing the life of the Spirit of love. It
is relevant here to recall the words of the High-Priestly prayer

of our Lord that the goal of the *ekklesia* is its perfected unity for
the sake of winning the world.   God has been building up a
Christian fellowship which now exists in every nation; and
this world Church is the basis of our hope that one day all the
nations shall be diadems in the crown of our enthroned and
universal Lord.   The goal must ultimately be in the world to
come.   An innumerable company shall be gathered around
the throne of God ((Rev 7₉, ₁₄, ₁₇); Christ will not be ashamed
to call us brethren (Heb 2₁₁).   It is this eternal background
and this divine quality which give *koinōnia* such a hopeful
significance.

Eight

'THE EXCEEDING GREATNESS OF HIS POWER'
(Ephesians 1₁₉)

In these days of frustration and disappointment it is an exceedingly inspiring experience to meditate on an illuminating
prayer recorded in Eph 1₁₉₋₂₀: 'That ye may know. . . . the
exceeding greatness of His power (δύναμις: *dunamis*) to usward
who believe, according to the working (ἐνέργεια: *energeia*) of
the strength (κράτος: *kratos*) of His might (ἰσχύς: *ischus*)
which He wrought in Christ when He raised Him from the
dead and made Him sit at His right hand in the heavenly
places.'   This statement is a veritable gold-mine, full of rich
and valuable treasure.   Nearly every word is priceless in its
spiritual suggestiveness.   There are no less than four remarkable Greek terms for 'power' in it.

   (i)   δύναμις (*dunamis*) is the term from which our word
'dynamite' is derived.   It occurs over one hundred times in
the New Testament.   When Paul was writing to the Christians
at Rome, he used the word: 'I am not ashamed of the Gospel;
for it is the *power* of God unto salvation to everyone that be-
lieveth' (Ro 1₁₆).   The capital city of the great Pagan Empire
was a cesspool of iniquity.   The words of the poet were only
too true:

On that hard Roman World
Disgust and secret loathing fell;
Deep weariness and sated lust
Made human life a hell.

There were 330,000 on the dole and one-third of the population were slaves. The spectacle of human bloodshed in the famous gladiatorial games was one of the chief amusements. The combats of blindfolded men, dwarfs and deformed people aroused only the happiest feelings. Yet, in spite of the towering edifice of evil custom and vice, Paul was confident that the Gospel had the power to cause the mighty fabric to collapse. When Constantine the Great sought the best way of infusing new blood into the empire, he discovered that Christianity was the answer; and that was done when the Christians numbered only three millions in a population of sixty millions!

(ii) The second word for power in Ephesians (chapter 1) is ἐνέργεια (*energeia*). It is found in the papyri in reference to a mill. It literally means 'inworking' and suggests the inward propulsion of power. The same word is used about the fashioning of the body of our humiliation, so that it may be conformed to the body of Christ's glory, 'according to the working (ἐνέργειαν: *energeian*) whereby He is able to subdue all things to Himself' (Ph 3₂₁). 'Love, joy, peace, long-suffering, kindness, goodness, faithfulness, meekness, self-control' are produced by the vital life of the Holy Spirit, just as truly as the marvellous chemistry and power of a tree make it laden with fruit. 'All of us who are Christians have no veils on our faces, but reflect like mirrors the glory of the Lord. We are transfigured by the Spirit of the Lord in ever-increasing splendour into His own image' (*Letter to Young Churches*; 2 Co 3₁₈).

(iii) The third Greek word for power is κράτος (*kratos*). It suggests ability to conquer. 'Caesar saved Cleopatra's life', says an early papyrus, 'when he *conquered* (the same word) her kingdom.' Again, it is *kratos* which is reproduced in English in 'autocrat' and 'democrat'. In G. F. Watts' statue of 'Physical Energy' we have the figure of a powerful rider mounted on a magnificent horse. Though the high-spirited animal is, as it were, curvetting and prancing, yet it is kept securely under control. The knotted muscles and the tense sinews of the rider are well suggested. James in his Epistle emphasized the worthlessness of a man's religion if he does not bridle his tongue (Ja 1₂₆):

> *Unless above himself he can*
> *Erect himself, how poor a thing is man!*

(iv)   A fourth Greek word for power is found in the opening chapter of Ephesians. *Ἰσχύς (ischus)* was used in early times in reference to physical force. We come across the term in a papyrus: 'I was not strong enough to hinder him.' Paul uses the word in the great affirmation: 'I can do (*ἰσχύω: ischuō*) all things in Him that strengtheneth me' (Ph 4₁₃). When the Ephesian magicians had consigned their star-reading parchment rolls and spells to the flames, Luke made this comment: 'So mightily grew the word of the Lord and prevailed' (*ἴσχυεν: ischuen*)—Ac 19₂₀.

Nine

'MOVED BY THE HOLY GHOST'
(2 Peter 1₂₁)

AN interesting line of thought is formed in linking up three picturesque words which have a maritime association.

(1)   The Greek word *λειτουργία (leitourgia)*, from which our term 'liturgy' is derived, is used in its verbal form concerning the service which is rendered to God in public worship. The papyri reveal that it was associated with sacerdotal ministrations of the Egyptian priesthood.

But it must not be thought that the term had only that connotation. Though always connected with the idea of service, it had nevertheless a wide variety of applications. For instance, it was used about EQUIPPING A NAVAL VESSEL. Now when we bear in mind that *λειτουργία (leitourgia)* was associated with worship (the **cognate verb** is found in Ac 13₂) and when we recall that the literal meaning of the word is derived from *laos* (people) and *ergon* (work), it is reasonable to interpret the passage in Ac 13₂ as an equipment for service. Worship enables those who adore God to receive divine power and guidance, so that as Church members leave the Church they go forth commissioned to attack the forces of evil. It was in a church service at Antioch that Saul and Barnabas were impelled and guided by the Holy Spirit to go forth on a missionary journey that was full of amazing adventures, daring exploits and thrilling victories. Our Lord said that 'The gates of hell shall not prevail (κατισχύω: *katischuō*) against it' (the Church); and the Acts of the Apostles unfolds a glorious record of victories over the most relentless foes. 'So mightily grew the word of God and prevailed' (ἰσχύω: *ischuō*) (Ac 19₂₀).

Πλήρωμα (*plērōma*), which we have already recognized as having the meaning 'the full strength' of a naval vessel, suggests the thought that it is the Divine intention that Christ should fully dwell in and equip the Church. Many a worshipper has gone forth from Church filled with the Spirit of God, and commissioned to attack the insidious vested interests that batten on weak-willed men and women.

(2) There is another Greek word which reminds us that every dedicated life can have great assurance of Divine support. In the Epistle to the Hebrews we read that the heroes of faith '*greeted* (ἀσπάζομαι: *aspazomai*) *the promises* from afar and confessed that they were strangers and pilgrims on the earth' (He 11₁₃). 'Ασπάζομαι (*aspazomai*) was used about saluting ships at sea. Like passengers that have been crossing the ocean and later wave their handkerchiefs to the friends who are waiting to welcome them, so believers who witness for Christ in this materialistic world are tremendously enheartened as they gain a glimpse of the precious promises of God. The victory for their Master is more than won. The perils will soon be over and the Kingdom shall come (1 Co 15₂₅₋₂₆).

(3) A third picturesque word also reminds us of the sea. On the historic day of Pentecost 'suddenly there came from heaven a sound as of the rushing of a mighty wind' (Ac 2₂). This could literally be translated: 'A sound as of a mighty wind borne along' (φερομένης: *pheromenēs*). The same **verb** is used

in the well-known statement: 'Men speak from God, being moved (*borne along*) *by the Holy Ghost*' (2 P 1₂₁).

The marvellous transformation of the disciples after the pouring out of the Holy Spirit was a demonstration of power. They were borne along by the all-powerful influence of the Holy Spirit. The Greek word for 'Spirit' (πνεῦμα: *pneuma*) can also be translated 'wind'. Similarly the Hebrew word— 'ruach'—meant the 'Spirit' and also the powerful wind of the desert. Every yachtsman knows that however favourable the wind may be, it will not bear the yacht out to sea unless the anchor is pulled up and the sails hoisted. What happened in the early Church was that the members unloosed the moorings and raised their sails; then the wind of the Holy Spirit bore them along. When Christians put the emphasis today on prayer and faith, miracles will be repeated. However invisible and mysterious a thing be the wind, it can be felt and its power proved.

The writer of the Epistle to the Hebrews refers to the danger of being swept along past the sure anchorage which is within reach. There are currents of opinion, habit, tradition and convention which tend to carry us away insensibly from the course which we should keep. 'Therefore, we ought to give the more earnest heed to the things that were heard', says a New Testament writer, 'lest haply we drift away (παραρυῶμεν: *pararuōmen*) from them' (He 2₁). Παραρρέω (*pararreō*) had many interesting associations in early times. Plutarch used it of things like a ring which slips off the finger. Aristotle employed it in reference to a crumb of bread which took a wrong course and got into the windpipe. Origen mentioned it when writing about DRIFTING from religious duties.

This is the sense in which the Revised Version translates the word. The urgency of taking heed to the possibility of drifting is apparent inasmuch as drifting is (*a*) imperceptible; (*b*) easy; and (*c*) perilous. The secret of avoiding a disastrous voyage is suggested in the words of a great Highland mystic: 'When thou art low, make but a little cry to God, and thou shalt find Him in thy heart, and all the powers of heaven at thy hand.'

Ten

'HE IS ABLE TO SUCCOUR THEM THAT ARE TEMPTED'

(Hebrews 2₁₈)

THE word πειράζω (*peirazō*), or the **noun** πειρασμός (*peiras-mos*) mentioned in Mt 6₁₃ and 26₄₁, or ἐκπειράζω (*ekpeirazō*; Lk 10₂₅, Mt 4₇) has a wide range of meaning. It signifies (*a*) to attempt; (*b*) to test or prove the quality of a man or instrument; and (*c*) to seduce to evil. When our Lord said, 'Ye are they which have continued with Me in My tempta-tions', He meant His 'trials', as Moffatt translates *peirasmois* (Lk 22₂₈). But 'Everyone is tempted,' says St James, 'when drawn away (ἐξελκόμενος: *exelkomenos*) by his own lust (ἐπιθυμίας: *epithumias*) and enticed' (δελεαζόμενος: *deleazo-menos*)—Ja 1₁₄. The **first verb** in this passage signifies 'drag-ging along' and was used of a crocodile which was captured with a noose. The **second verb** means 'enticed with a bait'. What is the fisherman's bait in this case? The word trans-lated 'lust' is used of a vague craving for something not yet articulate. We find the word in a papyrus regarding a hus-band who longs to be with his wife who has forsaken him. Though at times the restless man may seek after wealth, pleasure and ease; yet, he may come to make the discovery: 'I know now what I really need to make me secure.' On the other hand, someone may come to realize that he has been drawn away by lower impulses. He sees the bait and is en-ticed. Disappointment and frustration bring the unpleasant fact home to him.

We have already noticed βοηθέω (*boētheō*) which is used of running to the help of someone in need (Mt 15₂₅). It is also found in the great passage in He 2₁₈: 'For in that He Himself hath suffered being tempted, He is able to succour (βοηθῆσαι: *boēthēsai*) them that are tempted.' The **aorist** suggests the single, momentary act of coming to help. Westcott points out, 'The phrase expresses more than the simple fact (βοηθει: *boēthei*). Only one who has learnt by suffering can rightly feel with another in his sufferings. . . .   The power of sympathy lies not in the mere capacity for feeling, but in the lessons of experience.   Again, sympathy with the sinner in his trial does not depend on the experience of sin but on the experience of the strength of the temptation to sin which only the sinless can know in full intensity.   He who falls yields before the last strain.   Sin dulls sympathy by obscuring the idea of evil.' As the papyri reveal, we are not warranted in drawing too fine a distinction between κοινωνέω (koinōneō) and μετέχω (metechō) (He 2₁₄), though some commentators would affirm that the former suggests personal fellowship and the latter participation in some common privilege.   Jesus Himself shared our flesh and blood and knew how strong were the promptings to commit sin.

It is instructive to observe the order of the Greek words which are translated in our RV: 'But God is faithful, who will not suffer you to be tempted above that ye are able: but will with the temptation make also the way of escape (ἔκβασις: ekbasis), that ye may be able to endure (ὑπενεγκεῖν: hupenegkein) it' (1 Co 10₁₃).   Πιστός (pistos) is written first, as if to emphasize that however sore the trial may be, the believer can rest on the rock of God's faithfulness.   Ἔκβασις (ekbasis) means an exit from a mountain pass.   We can picture an adventurous band of people penned overnight by the enemy in a narrow defile, with every means of egress apparently sealed. Yet, in the morning, a way of exit has been discovered and the perilous situation is relieved.   We recall an early gloss on a phrase in the Lord's Prayer—'Lead us not into temptation which we cannot bear.'   Yet Paul is confident that the best release from temptation is found in the power to endure.   Then a man can be more than a conqueror.   He has not only overcome the trial but he has actually acquired the sterling quality of endurance.   Ὑποφέρω (hupopherō) literally means 'bearing up under a load'.   It is a masculine word suggesting heroic loyalty and confidence.   The trial will end in victory.

Rev. W. W. Gauld suggests (in The Expository Times, June 1941) that ἔκβασις (ekbasis) may not only mean 'a way of escape' from a difficult mountainous country, but also disembarking after a perilous voyage.   'A tiny craft, apparently doomed to shipwreck on an unbroken line of cliff, suddenly, and to the inexperienced landsman, unexpectedly, slips through a gap on the inhospitable coast into security and peace.' The ancients looked with fear on the sea and would understand Chrysostom's reference to 'the unfathomable main' and 'the yawning depths' of the storm-tossed water. To the believer who lives in Christ there is a great security. When he is renewed the whole bent of his nature is away from sin. 'Whosoever is begotten of God doeth no sin, because his seed abideth in him; and he cannot sin because he is begotten of God' (1 Jn 3₉). If sin is committed, the reference must be to an occasional act of sin; but the **tenses** that are used in St John's first Epistle remind us that the author draws a distinction between an occasional lapse and habitual sin or a continuous sinful state. As long as a man's relationship with Christ is real, sinful acts are but as accidents; the central citadel of his being is impregnable. 'Whosoever is begotten of God sinneth not; but He that was begotten of God keepeth him, and the evil one toucheth (ἅπεται: *hapetai*) him not' (1 Jn 5₁₈). The Greek word here suggests 'a laying hold of', and not a mere superficial touch. It is used in the papyri in the active sense of 'kindling' or 'setting fire to' certain things. If the evil one is aggressive, there is a Divine Guardian who keeps us secure. It is our faith that gives us the victory (1 Jn 5₄).

We may sum up the subject under three divisions:

(1)   THE CHALLENGE of temptation.

> *When the fight begins,*
> *A man's worth something.   God stoops o'er his head,*
> *Satan looks up between his feet—both tug—*
> *. . . The soul waits and grows.*

(2)   THE CONTROL of temptation. God will not suffer any temptation beyond our power of endurance. There is a limit to what He allows.

(3)   THE CONQUEST of temptation. To those who trust God, adequate power will be given to withstand the strain and shock. The confidence of the believer is founded on the rock of God's faithfulness (1 Co 10₁₃).

Eleven

'ALL HAVE SINNED AND FALL SHORT OF THE GLORY OF GOD'

(Romans 3₂₃)

SOMEONE has said that we confess small sins in order to in-sinuate that we have no great ones. But Paul who had been a very zealous Pharisee said: 'All have sinned and fall short (ὑστεροῦνται: *husterountai*) of the glory of God' (Ro 3₂₃). This Greek **verb** is translated elsewhere 'be destitute' or 'be in want'. It is the same word that is used to describe the Prodigal's condition in the far country—involving want, waste, and wilfulness. Alienation from God produces the same waste and want today.

Archbishop Trench (in his *New Testament Synonyms*) sums up a striking catalogue of words for sin: 'Sin may be regarded as the missing of a mark—it is then ἁμαρτία (*hamartia*); the over-passing or transgressing of a line—it is then παράβασις (*parabasis*); the disobedience to a voice—in that case it is παρακοή (*parakoe*); the falling where one should have stood upright—this will be παράπτωμα (*paraptōma*); ignorance of what one ought to have known—this will be ἀγνόημα (*agnoēma*); diminishing of that which should have been rendered in full measure, which is ἥττημα (*hettema*); non-observance of a law which is ἀνομιά (*anomia*).' The other word which he mentions: πλημμέλεια (*plemmeleia*), meaning a discord in the harmonies of God's universe, is not found in the New Testament, but it occurs in the Septuagint translation of the Books of Leviticus and Numbers.

> *Disproportionate sin*
> *Jarred against nature's chime, and with harsh din,*
> *Broke the fair music that all creatures made*
> *To their great Lord.*

If sin is compared to discord, it is worthy of notice that on the return of the Prodigal to his home there was music (συμφωνιά: *sumphōnia*)—Lk 15₂₅. Whenever the soul experiences the healing fact of forgiveness and reconciliation with God there is harmony and peace (Isaiah 53₅). *Sumphōnia* is found in the papyri with the sense of 'music' and also 'agreement'.

The most frequently used term to describe sin in the New Testament is ἁμαρτία (hamartia). This word also is found in an early papyrus in reference to a boy's appeal to his mother for forgiveness. 'I know that I have sinned', he says. Homer used the word to describe the failure of a warrior to strike his foe with his spear. We find hamartia also in one of Aristotle's writings regarding a poet who did not treat his subject poetically. Sin is a tragic blunder, a failure to attain the true end of our lives—to know Jesus, to be perfect in love and to be one in fellowship. The arrow that misses the mark wounds the heart of God.

(i) St Paul speaks of people being 'alienated (ἀπηλλοτρι-ωμένοι: apellōtriōmenoi) from the life of God' (Eph 4₁₈). The Greek word is found in the papyri in reference to an *estrangement* between parents. We can never afford to overlook the personal relationship involved between God and the human soul. Our Creator made man in His own image and capable of having fellowship with God. But man has rebelled against God, even (as someone has said) if his rebellion sometimes takes the form of indifference to the claims of God upon him. Oftentimes it reveals itself most tragically in the refusal of that love wherewith God seeks to draw the sinner to Himself.

(ii) Sin incurs a *debt*. A reference is made to it in the Lord's Prayer (Mt 6₁₂) and in certain parables. Ὀφείλημα (opheilēma) is a word full of dark suggestiveness for the sinner. The man who lives a respectable moral life and knows no experience of that overwhelming sense of gratitude which he owes to Him Who came to pardon him—even he misses the essential thing in the Christian religion. We owe to God our love which should abound towards all others, whom He has created and continues to love.

(iii) Sin not only incurs estrangement and a debt, but it also causes us to fall into *bondage*. The evil one makes us his slaves and the militant enemy captures us as prisoners. It is a bondage of corruption (Ro 8₂₁). 'The wages (ὀψώνια: opsōnia) of sin is death' (Ro 6₂₃). The Greek word was used in early days for a soldier's pay. It is mentioned in certain papyri. It originally represented the small allowance made to a combatant to purchase relish (*opson*) for consuming with his rations. Sin is a cruel tyrant, whose only reward is death.

It is recorded in the papyri that a man broke off the engagement of his daughter to a certain Phoebammon because the latter was involved in 'lawless deeds'. The same term (ἄθεσμος: *athesmos*) is found in 2 P 2₇ and 3₁₇. When the self-assertive will of man clashes with the will of a holy, wise and loving God the moral law is transgressed with disastrous consequences. This idea is further illustrated by the use of ἐκκλίνω (*ekklinō*) which means to bend away from or turn aside. 'They have all turned aside (εξέκλιναν: *exeklinan*), they are become unprofitable (ἠχρεώθησαν: *echreōthēsan*); there is none that doeth good, no, not so much as one' (Ro 3₁₂). The **verb** translated 'become unprofitable' means to 'go bad', like sour milk. Yet another aspect of the effect of sin is seen in being made 'weak' (ἀσθενής: *asthenēs*) or 'sickly' (Ro 5₆). The **derivative verb** is used in the papyri with the meaning of being 'in a sorry plight' or being 'impoverished'. The sinner is in a helpless condition. He is unable to redirect his will toward divine ends. The more he sins the less conscious is he of his sin. Κακός (*kakos*) usually indicates what is essentially evil in character. Πονηρός (*ponēros*) denotes evil that causes toil, pain and sorrow. Both words are associated with evil thoughts (Mt 15₁₉, Mk 7₂₁).

Sin blinds its victims and they cannot see where they are going. 'He that hateth his brother is in the darkness, and walketh in the darkness, and knoweth not whither he goeth (ὑπάγει: *hupagei*), because the darkness hath blinded (ἐτύφλωσεν: *etuphlōsen*) his eyes' (1 Jn 2₁₁). Westcott, commenting on ὑπάγει (*hupagei*), says: 'The idea is not that of proceeding to a definite point (πορεύομαι: *poreuomai*), but of leaving the present scene.' The power of evil is such that rich people are so blinded by their success that they do not see where they are going. The organ of spiritual sight becomes atrophied. When hatred dominates a person's life and he regards others as vermin, he is in spiritual darkness and knows not that he is heading for a disastrous end.

We read in 1 Ti 4₂ (RVm) about people being 'seared (κεκαυστηριασμένων: *kekausteriasmenōn*) in their own conscience'. Just as a burnt hand loses the sense of touch, so the evil conscience is cauterized. It does not realize the eternal values. Another impressive metaphor is mentioned in Titus 1₁₅ where there is a reference to the defiling effect of sin. Μιαίνειν (*miainein*) literally means 'to stain with colour', then to defile or pollute. Another Greek word which is translated 'defile' (μολύνειν: *molunein*) in 1 Co 8₇ and Rev 3₄ means besmearing with mud or filth. Aristotle speaks of swine besmearing themselves. Yet a third word, σπιλοῦν (*spiloun*), signifies 'to make a stain' and so 'defile'. James uses it about the tongue staining the whole body (Ja 3₆). What a grim catalogue of sins is outlined in Mark's Gospel, as our Lord sets forth the things which defile a man (Mk 7₂₂). It will be observed that these sins destroy the spirit of fellowship with others, whom God loves as much as He loves us. We can never separate our love for others from our love for Christ.

So lofty is the standard expected of us and so feeble and infected is man's will that the experience of one who was a zealous and worthy Pharisee is not an isolated case: 'O wretched (ταλαίπωρος: *talaipōros*) man that I am! who shall deliver me out of this body of death?' (Ro 7₂₄). There was a tyrant called Mezentius who punished his victims by attaching dead bodies to them. Vergil tells us that a murderer had the same fate meted out to him. Wherever the living man went he carried this body of corruption, its face opposite his face. It was a miserable experience. He was under the control of a tyrant. His struggles were in vain. How he longed for deliverance! He himself could never meet the moral demands of God.

Twelve

'NOT FIT FOR THE KINGDOM'
(Luke 9₆₂)

OUR Lord said: 'No man having put his hand to the plough and looking back is fit (εὔθετος: *euthetos*) for the Kingdom of God' (Lk 9₆₂). This Greek word (which literally means 'well-placed') implies that such a man is not adapted for the kind of service which Christ expects. The term is used about a person who is unsuitable for some official position; and it is the same word that is associated with our Lord's statement about salt that has lost its savour: 'It is fit (εὔθετον: *eutheton*) neither for the land, nor for the dunghill; men cast it out.' The soldier who is half-hearted and cowardly in a critical moment, the merchant who is more prone to indulge in sport than to be absorbed in his business and the church member who gives lip service to God on Sunday but who compromises with the world on Monday are all no use. No religion is worth anything that is not a passion.

It has puzzled some readers of the New Testament why Jesus said: 'All ye shall be offended: for it is written, I will smite the shepherd, and the sheep shall be scattered abroad' (Mk 14₂₇).

Σκανδαλίζω (*skandalizō*) is translated 'caused to stumble' in the RVm. After much inquiry into the general use of this word, it is suggested that the meaning is 'set a trap for', rather than 'put a stumbling-block in the way of'. The **noun** in Greek is the name for the lever in a trap, upon which the bait is put. When the animal touches it, the trap goes off and the animal is caught. Nobody likes to be taken in, or caught in a trap; hence in that sense a man may 'be offended'. Christ in the above passage is warning the disciples that they will be taken off their guard and surprised. The terrible shock that came to them when their Master was betrayed, denied and crucified proved that our Lord was correct in his prediction.

Paul warns the people at Colossae about false teachers: 'Take heed lest there be anyone that maketh spoil (συλαγωγῶν:

sulagōgōn) of you through his philosophy and vain deceit' (Col 2₈). The picture here is not that of being robbed but of being dragged off into slavery. Paul sees the converts being captured and led away with a cord round their necks, like the long strings of captives on the Assyrian monuments.

One of the alarming facts of life today is that great evils like gambling have become commercialized. Groups of selfish men have banded themselves together to batten on human weakness and make themselves immensely rich through the downfall of weak-willed men and women. Paul uses a significant phrase in Eph 4₁₉ about hard-hearted Gentiles: They 'gave themselves up . . . to work (ἐργασίαν: *ergasian*) all uncleanness with greediness' (πλεονεξία:: *pleonexia*). We find *ergasia* used in the papyri for 'making a trade of' and *pleonexia* is the word for 'covetousness': yet sometimes it has a wider range of meaning. It stands for that self-assertive spirit which disregards the rights of others.

Paul calls covetousness 'idolatry' (Col 3₅) and puts the covetous man side by side with fornicators (1 Co 5₁₀). The man who worships the Goddess of Luck cannot believe at the same time in the God and Father of our Lord Jesus Christ. 'My little children,' said John, 'guard yourselves from idols' (ἐιδώλων: *eidōlon*) (1 Jn 5₂₁). This Greek word always suggests unreality. Plato uses it in reference to illusory phenomena or appearances which are contrasted with eternal verities. In the Septuagint the same word is applied to the counterfeit gods of the heathen. The application of the term in the New Testament must be to pagan practices in social life. False ideas of God would have to be opposed. There must be no compromise. We live in an age of god-makers. Narcissus, the fair son of a river-god, fell in love with his own reflection in a pool: and selfishness is still the religion of many today. Who can deny, too, that Mars (the god of war), Bacchus (the god of wine), Venus (the goddess of love), Apollo (the god of physical beauty) and Minerva (the goddess of science) are still the real gods of many people? Every day we are reminded of the adoration of the blind goddess, Fortuna, holding a wheel as the symbol of her fickleness and instability. And then, there is the remaking of the

Golden Calf! Is not the worship of it one of the major sins today?

The disastrous consequences of disowning Christ are indicated in a picturesque word in 2 P 3₁₇: 'Beware lest ye fall away (ἐκπέσητε: *ekpesēte*) from your own steadfastness.' This is the very **verb** that is used in Acts 27₁₇ about the 'falling into' or 'unto' perilous quicksands. Eventually the ship was wrecked after it was 'cast upon' (the same **verb**) a certain island (Acts 27₂₆). Two **strong verbs** are found in a familiar rhetorical question—'What is a man profited, if he gain the whole world and lose (ἀπολέσας: *apolesas*) or forfeit (ζημιωθείς: *zēmiōtheis*) his own soul?' (Lk 9₂₅). Ἀπόλλυμι (*apollumi*) is used by Greek writers in the sense of 'utterly destroying', such as in the case of soldiers who are killed in battle or of buildings which are consumed by flames. Ζημιόω (*zēmioō*) is found with the meaning 'receiving damage' or 'suffering loss'. Life is forfeited. The man who loses his soul, loses the enjoyment of fellowship with Christ, the testimony of a good conscience and the reward of eternal felicity in heaven. There is a striking contrast between the man who forfeits his soul for the transient pleasures of the world and the man who having found Christ (the pearl of great price) willingly 'suffers the loss (ἐζημιώθην: *ezēmiothēn*) of all things' (Ph 3₈).

The unrenewed life is spoken of as 'the old man which waxeth corrupt (τὸν φθειρόμενον: *ton phtheiromenon*) after the lusts of deceit' (Eph 4₂₂). Φθείρω (*phtheirō*) suggests destruction through corruption. Just as the body of a motor car can be slowly destroyed through the effect of rust working in unseen parts, so man's nature can be ruined because of the effect of sinful impulses, evil thoughts and deceitful passions.

This process is made more pitiable because man's God-given powers become atrophied. Darkness settles down (ἐσκοτίσθη: *eskotisthē*) on all the faculties (Ro 1₂₁). Men become wilfully blind to the evidences of God and sink into idolatry. How could a traitor be expected to serve the King he disowns?

Thirteen

'HE CARRIED UP OUR SINS TO THE TREE'

(1 Peter 2₂₄)

THE RV Marginal Reading of 1 P 2₂₄ translates ἐπὶ τὸ ξύλον (*epi to xulon*) 'to the tree'. Jesus went deliberately to the Cross. He laid down His life of Himself (Jn 10₁₈). Each of the three Synoptists informs us that Jesus when on the Cross cried with a loud voice (φωνὴν μεγάλην: *phōnen megalēn*)—Mk 15₃₇; Mt 27₅₀; Lk23₄₆. It was the triumphant note of a conqueror. The Fourth Evangelist tells us the content of that mighty cry—'It is finished' (τετέλεσται: *tetelestai*)—Jn 19₃₀. It is the same word which Jesus had shortly before used when He said: 'Knowing that all things are now finished (τετέλεσται: *tetelestai*)—Jn 19₂₈; all that the prophets had foretold was fulfilled, all that His Father had sent Him to accomplish had been done, sin was fought to a finish and He Himself had overcome the world.

'He bowed (κλίνας: *klinas*) His head, and gave up His spirit' (Jn 19₃₀). The same **verb** is used about the Son of Man who had 'not where to lay (κλίνη: *klinē*) His head' (Lk 9₅₈). As W. E. Vine says (in *An Expository Dictionary of New Testament Words*), 'What is indicated in the statement "He bowed His head" is not the helpless dropping of the head after death, but the deliberate putting of His head into a position of rest. He died while we were yet sinners. He took the initiative and wrought a wondrous victory. The Cross is an expression in time of what took place in eternity. We thereby see into the heart of God. Man by his idolatry could have been left to suffer the consequences of his own sin; but God's love could not tolerate a corrupt society being left to its own awful doom. He—and He alone and of His own free-will—came to the rescue. He would not be satisfied with giving helpful advice. God must tabernacle in human flesh and die, the righteous for the unrighteous, that He might bring us to God' (1 P 3₁₈).

The word 'Atonement' (καταλλαγή: *katallagē*) in Ro 5₁₁ (AV) should more correctly be translated 'reconciliation' as in the RV. Writing to the Corinthians, Paul says, 'God was in Christ, reconciling the world unto Himself' (2 Co 5₁₉). Καταλλάσσω (*katallassō*) means properly 'to exchange coins', then to change people from hatred to friendship. In the New Testament God is never referred to as having to be reconciled. It is rebellious man who is called upon to change his attitude and to accept the forgiving grace which God in Christ has so lovingly provided. All the barriers to reconciliation are in man; and, as Dr C. Ryder Smith says in *The Grace of the Lord Jesus Christ* (Epworth Press): 'Man can only be changed if God's sympathy with a sinner is so intense that He puts Himself where the sinner is. He did this on the Cross.' This new relationship between God and the penitent sinner is one of peace. The old enmity is gone.

'For if, while we were enemies (ἐχθροί: *echthroi*), we were reconciled (κατηλλάγημεν: *katēllagēmen*) to God through the death of His Son, much more being reconciled shall we be saved by His life (ἐν τῇ ζωῇ αὐτοῦ), Ro 5₁₀. Though God recognizes the hostility of men ('enemies'), yet His love never loses its patience. Whilst many New Testament writers believed in the Old Testament conception of 'the wrath of God', e.g., Ro 5₉, they did not regard it as a capricious or unjust attribute. 'The wrath of God' is a process whereby sin brings about disastrous consequences. 'For he that soweth unto his own flesh, shall of the flesh reap corruption' (φθοράν: *phthoran*). This last word—φθορά (*phthora*) (found in Gal 6₈)—is found in the papyri with the meaning 'decay'. The sinner becomes so enfeebled in his will that he cannot stop the rot that has set in in his soul. Similarly with the Roman Empire, it was the moral corruption that caused it to perish (Gibbon).

Now, it is helpful to observe a few Greek words here. Σώζειν (*sōzein*)—'to save'—has early medical associations. Though θεραπεύειν (*therapeuein*) and ἰάσθαι (*iasthai*) are translated 'to heal' in the New Testament, σώζειν (*sōzein*) is also used. We read, for example (in Lk 8₃₆), 'They also that saw it told them how he that was possessed with demons was saved (RVm). Christ can still save people from the distressing consequences of the demons of irrational fears, neurasthenia, unconscious guilt, melancholia, alcoholism and sex perversions. It is important to realize how well-known psychologists have come to see that the Christian Religion is as indispensable as it is effective in 'saving' people's lives.

The second Greek word which we wish to notice in this connexion is ἱλαστήριον (hilasterion)—'propitiation'. 'Whom (i.e. Jesus Christ) God purposed to be propitiatory through faith in His blood, to show His righteousness (δικαιοσύνης: dikaiosunēs), because of the passing over (πάρεσιν: paresin) of the sins done aforetime, in the forbearance of God' (Ro 3₂₅ RVm). Dr C. H. Dodd points out (*The Moffatt New Testament Commentary*, p. 54) that the translating of *hilasterion* as 'propitiation' is misleading, for it suggests the placating of an angry God. Though pagan religions used the word in that sense, the writers of the Bible avoided the idea. 'It is God Who puts forward the means whereby the guilt of sin is removed, by sending Christ'; the word therefore carries with it the idea—'a means by which sin is forgiven'. As sin was regarded as a defilement or a moral taint, 'propitiation' in Old Testament times referred to certain ritual acts (such as the sprinkling of blood) which acted as a kind of disinfectant (compare Isaiah 53₄, ₅). As time advanced, it was recognized that only God could really remove sin. 'He is the propitiation (ἱλασμός: hilasmos) for our sins' (1 Jn 2₂). 'The blood of Jesus Christ His Son cleanseth (καθαρίζει: katharizei) us from all sin (1 Jn 1₇). Sin is forgiven and removed. The 'means of expiation' was at work in the sacrifice of Him Who united two natures in one. The word 'Jesus' reminds us of how the efficacy of Christ's blood can be imparted to us, whilst the term, 'His Son', brings out the idea that there was a Divine action and value in it. 'His blood can make the foulest clean.' The evil taint is gone and the forgiven sinner is ready for grateful service.

Fourteen

'MADE WHITE IN THE BLOOD
OF THE LAMB'
(Revelation 7₁₄)

THE word αἷμα (*haima*)—blood—has a very important spiritual significance. Blood symbolizes the life. The Jews in post-Exilic times identified the shedding of the blood of an animal with the offering up of the most precious thing they possessed —their lives. Similarly, later generations spoke of the blood of Christ as representing His life as offered up in dedication to God. The word blood is connected with Christ's death over thirty times in the apostolic writings. Sometimes it is by the blood of Christ that believers are 'purchased' (Ac 20₂₈; 1 P 1₁₈₋₁₉) or 'ransomed' (Eph 1₇) or 'loosed' (Rev 1₅).

But the question may be asked: Why did Jesus use the word 'blood' in the phrase, 'My blood of the covenant which is shed for (ὑπέρ: *huper*) many' (Mk 14₂₄)? We read in Ex 24₈ that after some oxen had been sacrificed their blood was sprinkled both on the altar and on the people; and Moses said, 'Behold the blood of the covenant, which the Lord hath made with you upon all these conditions'. In this covenant the people were pledged to God and He to them for ever. The conditions of the covenant were contained in the Book of the Law. When Jeremiah described a new covenant, he meant it was to be no longer imposed from without but experienced from within. 'They shall all know Me, from the least of them unto the greatest' (Jer 31₃₁₋₃₄). It is a remarkable fact how all through the Scriptures blood is associated with unity or fellowship. Jesus by His death drew men not only to Himself but to one another. It is no accident that we find that lovely and intimate fellowship of the Church linked with the cleansing blood of Christ (1 Jn 1₇). Charles Wesley truly described the Church as the company 'of pardoned sinners'. All true believers today are 'of one heart and soul' (Ac 4₃₂).

On the great Day of Atonement the blood of the sacrificed oxen was sprinkled upon the altar to cleanse and hallow it

from the uncleanness of the children of Israel (Lv 16₁₉).   In
the New Testament we have four striking references to the
cleansing power of the blood—He 9₁₄; 1 P 1₂; 1 Jn 1₇; Rev 7₁₄.
In the Old Testament we have the gracious promise—'Though
your sins be as scarlet, they shall be as *white as snow*' (Is 1₁₈).
The same Greek word that is used in the Septuagint version
of that passage (λευκαίνω: *leukainō*) is also found in the well-
known words in Rev 7₁₄: 'they washed their robes and made
them white in the blood of the Lamb.'   Dr Ryder Smith
points out that 'washing in blood' is original with the Seer and
is derived from his experience that through the Death of
Christ bad men become good men.   Whilst πλύνω (*pluno*)
is used in this passage about 'washing robes', it is interesting
to note that in the papyri it was employed for cleansing the
tongue from bitterness.

Νίπτω (*niptō*)—another word for washing—almost invariably refers to the washing of a part of the body, while λούω
(*louō*) is used for the bathing of the whole body.   The contrast is clearly brought out in Jn 13₁₀: 'He that is bathed
(λελουμένος: *leloumenos*) needeth not save to wash (νίψασθαι:
nipsasthai) his feet, but is clean every whit.'   The guest was
expected to bathe (λούειν: *louein*) before attending a social
function; and accordingly, in the incident before us, the dust
had to be washed off the feet.   The foot-washing was sacramental as well as exemplary; and when Peter, who had at first
objected to the Lord washing his feet, realized the significance
of the act, he exclaimed: 'Lord, not my feet only, but also my
hands and my head.'   He wanted a cleansed nature.

Fifteen

'REMISSION OF SINS'

(Matthew 26₂₈)

'BEING justified (δικαιωθέντες: *dikaiōthentes*) by faith, let us
have peace with God through our Lord Jesus Christ' (Ro 5₁).
Many converts have rejoiced in the peace of conscience

which simple faith in a redeeming God has given to them.

'Forgiveness is a beggar's refuge', said Mr Bernard Shaw, 'we must pay our debts.' But no matter how much merit man seeks to accumulate he must always be a beggar. He can never repay his debt to God. He stands before the judge a guilty prisoner worthy of being shut out for ever from the presence of God with all the eternal felicities and fellowship of heaven. What a miracle is enshrined in this doctrine of Justification by faith! The Judge (who represents justice) declares the unjust innocent. The guilty one is acquitted, not because of any merit or because of anything he has done, but purely because of the free, kindly and arbitrary favour of the King. In the papyri δικαιόω (*dikaio-ō*) is found with the meaning 'to declare just'. Yet in Is 5₂₃ (see also Ex 23₇) woes are pronounced on those unjust judges who 'justify the wicked for a reward'. It was therefore a very unheard-of thing to attribute such an attitude to God to Whom 'righteousness' (δικαιοσύνη: *dikaiosunē*) meant the vindication of those who were wronged. This idea of the Greek word just quoted is clearly illustrated in the Old Testament.

But if it is a paradox for a Righteous Judge to acquit the guilty, rather than defend the wronged, we find that this metaphor of the law-court gives us insight in another direction. As C. H. Dodd says (*The Moffatt New Testament Commentary*, p. 52): 'It gave Paul the opportunity of emphasizing the sovereignty of God. When the prisoner has no case he throws himself on the mercy of the court. In this court the Judge is one whose will is law: if He acquits the prisoner, then he leaves the court without a stain on his character. It is all the doing of the God Who has reconciled me to Himself.'

Emerson said:

> Could'st thou in vision see
>   Thyself the man God meant,
> Thou never more could'st be
>   The man thou art content.

The commonest Greek word for 'remission of sins' is ἄφεσις (*aphesis*). It was variously illustrated in the papyri. It signified (i) the release of water from the sluices of canals for the purpose of *irrigation*.   One of the Prophets laments the desolation caused by the water-courses going dry (Jl 1₁₈₋₂₀).   It is a psychological fact that forgiveness has a liberating power. Where such an experience is lacking in the case of religious people, they become cranks and their lives are filled with discord and censoriousness.   Forgiveness has a healing influence. Ἄφεσις (*aphesis*) was also used for (ii) the '*release' of the harvest*, after the taxes had been paid.   Thereafter the farmers could make their own use of it.   Forgiveness involves an intimate experience between God and the penitent sinner.   But such forgiving love must be appropriated.   Paul could never forget that he 'obtained mercy' (1 Ti 1₁₃).   (iii) Ἄφεσις (*aphesis*) was used in inscriptions for '*remission of debt or punishment*'. Once again, we find it associated with (iv) the '*letting go' of the sacrificial dove* or scapegoat on the Day of Atonement, symbolizing the putting away of sin.   Paul refers to the 'passing over of the sins done aforetime, in the forbearance of God' (Ro 3₂₅).   The word πάρεσις (*paresis*) suggests the temporary suspension of punishment.   Every sin must at last be either forgiven or involve 'the wrath of God'; but at the Cross we realize the 'God-like miracle of love' in the overwhelming experience of a gracious forgiveness of all our sin.

Sixteen

'BOUGHT WITH A PRICE'
(1 Corinthians 6₂₀)

In an early papyrus we read of a prefect who addressed an accused man in court: 'Thou art worthy to be scourged, but I give you freely (χαρίζομαι: *charizomai*) to the multitude.' Paul takes this **verb** which was used about any person who had a kindly and gracious nature and applies it to the Divine attitude of forgiveness.   Indeed he links people's forgiveness of one another with God's forgiveness of them; and in each relationship this lovely verb is employed, thus implying that behind the act of forgiveness is a kindly nature (Eph 4₃₂).

In nothing was this kindly and sacrificial love more strikingly expressed than in the redemption wrought on Calvary. The foundations of the New Testament doctrine of redemption are lucidly indicated in an article in Hastings' *Dictionary of the Gospels* (p. 475). The Greek **verb** λυτρόω (*lutro-ō*) (see 1 P 1 $_{18-19}$) is used in reference to the deliverance of Israel from the Roman yoke (Lk 24$_{21}$). The **noun** λύτρον (*lutron*) is found in a papyrus in connexion with the purchase-money for manumitting slaves. The people of Israel had none of the social amenities that we have today. Certain laws had to be made such as that of the kinsman-redeemer. The latter had to redeem the mortgaged land of his dead friend. If the poor bankrupt had been forced by circumstances to sell himself as a slave, then it became the duty of the kinsman to pay for his freedom and settle his debts. 'Ye were bought: (ἠγοράσθητε: *ēgorasthēte*) with a price', said Paul (1 Co 6$_{20}$). Ἀγοράζω (*agorazō*) originally meant 'to frequent the market-place'; then 'to buy or sell' in it. It was used for buying out a slave with a view to giving him his freedom. Paul employs the **verb** about the deliverance of Christian Jews from the Law and its curse (Gal 3$_{13}$). Jesus thought of Himself as the Kinsman who set free those who were enslaved by sin by paying the price of His own life. He gave His 'life a ransom (λύτρον: *lutron*) for (ἀντί: *anti*) many' (Mk 10$_{45}$). Though it has been pointed out that ἀντί (*anti*) does not always denote substitution, Moulton and Milligan state that in the papyri the simple 'instead of' is by far the commonest meaning. It was a custom of old to surrender many soldiers as a means of ransoming a high military officer. In the case of Jesus it was the reverse; He gave His life a ransom for many.

The idea of redemption was linked up with the deliverance of the children of Israel from the house of bondage (Dt 7$_8$). It is remarkable that we find that the great deliverers of old (Moses and Elijah) spoke of 'the exodus' which Jesus was to accomplish at Jerusalem. Through a stupendous transaction which took place at Calvary Jesus 'broke through oppression' and 'set the captives free'.

In 1 Co 2$_8$ Paul makes reference to the rulers of this world crucifying Christ, hoping thereby to defeat the divine purpose;

but the apostle points out in Col 2₁₅ that what actually happened was that in the death of Christ God had vanquished them. This verse is a difficult one to translate; and though much can be said for the RV reading: 'having put off ($\dot{a}\pi\epsilon\kappa\delta\upsilon\sigma\acute{a}\mu\epsilon\nu\sigma\varsigma$: *apekdusamenos*) from Himself the principalities and powers' (that is, our human nature with all its temptations and conflicts), yet it is more in harmony with the metaphor which follows: 'triumphing over them'—to adopt the AV reading, 'having spoiled principalities and powers, He made a show of them openly, triumphing over them'.

Dr E. F. Scott, who prefers this rendering (*The Moffatt New Testament Commentary*), says: 'Christ is conceived of as doing battle with the great captains of that supernatural host which had enslaved the human race. He has beaten them down and stripped them of their armour, and then exposed them, by making a public spectacle—exhibiting them to men and angels as His captives.' The word for 'triumph' ($\theta\rho\iota\alpha\mu\beta\epsilon\acute{\upsilon}\omega$: *thriambeuō*) is a military metaphor, referring to the triumphal procession which followed a signal victory.

Seventeen

'A CANCELLED BOND'

(Colossians 2₁₄)

In a remarkable passage Paul says: (Christ) 'having blotted out ($\dot{\epsilon}\xi\alpha\lambda\epsilon\acute{\iota}\psi\alpha\varsigma$: *exaleipsas*) the bond ($\chi\epsilon\iota\rho\acute{o}\gamma\rho\alpha\phi\sigma\nu$: *cheirographon*) written in ordinances that was against us, which was contrary to us; and he hath taken it away, nailing it to the cross' (Col 2₁₄).

An old Oriental custom lies behind the metaphor here. When a debt had been settled either by payment or by forgiveness, the creditor took the cancelled bond and nailed it over the door of the house of the former debtor. Every passer-by would soon know the man was no longer in debt. It is beyond our capacity to pay the debt we owe to God. Jesus comes to a bankrupt world with a long list of our indebtedness to Him. He lifts it up where men and angels may see it; and as the nails go through His hands and feet, they go through the bond of our transgressions to cancel it for ever. (See Isaiah 43₂₅.)

Other commentators would see in the phraseology a reference to the custom of suspending over the head of a crucified victim the charge on which he had been condemned. Χειρόγραφον (*cheirographon*) meant an indictment drawn up against a prisoner, as well as a certificate of debt. If we adopt the former interpretation, then Paul views the Law (with its impossible ideals and severe penalties) as a veritable sentence of death against us. But Christ comes to our aid. To quote Col 2₁₄ (*Letters to Young Churches*): 'He has forgiven you all your sins; Christ has wiped out the damning evidence of broken laws and commandments which always hung over our heads, and has annulled it by nailing it over His own head on the Cross.'

It is an interesting thing that the **verb** αἴρω (*airō*) in the phrase 'He hath TAKEN IT AWAY' is used also in the familiar statement: 'Behold the Lamb of God which TAKETH AWAY the sin of the world' (Jn 1₂₉). It is found also in connexion with the boulder that was taken away from the entrance to the tomb of our Lord. By His death sin is removed; and by His Resurrection the obstacle to fellowship with our living Lord is also taken away. Death proved the gateway to life in its most resplendent form.

Looking back on the whole subject of the Atonement, we may select a few salient points. (i) He who has been alienated from God can be reconciled; (ii) he who has been weak-willed and tainted with the guilt of sin can find in Christ 'a propitiation' for his sin; (iii) he who has been in bondage to the evil one can be bought with Christ's precious blood; (iv) he who has incurred many a debt against his Creator can have all his past cancelled at the Cross. 'Hallelujah! What a Saviour!'

Eighteen

'THE NEW COVENANT'

(Luke 22$_{20}$)

THE word 'Covenant' occurs nearly three hundred times in the Bible. It has been variously interpreted as a mutual agreement, a binding ordinance or an obligation undertaken by a single person. The word 'bond' would cover most uses of it; for every covenant implies two parties. The sense of agreement was developed from a mere commercial transaction to a friendly relationship in which the uttermost loyalty is pledged. Such a bond is not unlike that between a husband and wife whose loyalty is pledged in love and whose trustfulness and unselfishness beautify the relationship. (i) God initiated a Covenant (Ex 6$_{5-7}$), He redeemed His people from Egypt (Hos 12$_9$), He is betrothed to Israel for ever (Hos 2$_{19}$), He is a faithful God Who will not fail succeeding generations (Dt 7$_9$); (ii) Man makes a covenant with others. Numerous references in Scripture indicate that this was solemnly accomplished (Gn 26$_{28}$; 1 S 18$_3$; 2 Ch 23$_1$, $_3$ etc.). In the light of the teaching of the New Testament, it is reasonable to find instances of men taking an oath to live on friendly terms, so that they may receive the Divine blessing. Covenants were often intensified by an oath and their violation was associated with the severest penalties (2 S 3$_{21-30}$); (iii) Man pledges his loyalty to God. As in marriage, the two parties 'pledge their troth either to other'. The prophets rose to a great height when they compared the relation of Jehovah to His people with that of a husband to his wife.

One of the outstanding passages in the whole Old Testament deals with the making of a new covenant (Jer 31$_{31-34}$). God will forgive the sins of His people and write His law on their hearts. It is a new (καινός: *kainos*) covenant. When something 'new' is contemplated under the aspect of time, it is καινός (*kainos*); whilst νέος (*neos*) signifies 'new' in quality. As Prof. Wheeler Robinson has said, the primary truths of this new bond are (*a*) the moral inwardness of true religion; (*b*) its dependence on supernatural agencies; and (c) its realization of a direct personal fellowship with God. When Jesus said: 'This cup is the new Covenant in My blood, even that which is poured out for you' (Lk 22₂₀), the emphasis is on the poured-out wine which symbolized His self-sacrifice and sealed the new Covenant. No longer would God's people safeguard their own interests by shedding the blood of others. They would shed their own blood. Knowing that Jesus had poured out His own blood on Calvary, they would gladly pledge their loyalty—even to the uttermost sacrifice—to Him Who had betrothed Himself to them.

The author of the Epistle to the Hebrews reminds us that the Death of Christ has a twofold aspect. His blood is not only the means of atonement, but the ratification of the Covenant which succeeded it. 'He is the mediator of a new Covenant', διαθήκης καινῆς μεσίτης (diathēkēs kainēs mesitēs)' (He 9₁₅). By His death Christ attested the inviolable force of the Covenant which He established. He made the new relation between God and man sure. Dr W. F. Howard says: 'Διαθήκη (diathēkē) was preferred to the classical συνθήκη (sunthēkē) as the regular translation of the Hebrew word for "covenant", because the **preposition** in the latter compound might suggest a contractual agreement made by equals.' Referring to the two meanings of διαθήκη (diathēkē) ('covenant' and 'will'), Dr Howard adds: 'Διαθήκη (diathēkē) is equivalent to the legal term "instrument"; in one case an instrument which God draws up and sends to His people to express His will; in the special sense of "instrument" suggesting a disposition made of property in view of ultimate death' (in *A Companion to the Bible*: Manson). So may we receive the promise of the eternal inheritance (He 9₁₅). Moses secured for the children of Israel a great inheritance; but it was but a faint foreshadowing of the rich provision made by Christ.

All believers are His own people and He is their God. His past dealings have always been a testimony to His faithfulness; and He still waits to enter into a covenant with those who, like Charles Kingsley, can affirm: 'I have devoted myself to God, a vow never, if He give me the faith I pray for, to be recalled.'

3

Nineteen

'LOVE YOUR ENEMIES'
(Matthew 5₄₄)

THE Greek word ἀγαπάω (*agapaō*), which was nurtured in the bosom of revealed religion, is used over two hundred and fifty times in the New Testament. It was preferred to ἔρως (*eros*) which was associated with sensuous lust. Though ἀγαπάω (*agapaō*) is often synonymous with φιλέω (*phileō*), it really represents something deeper. Indeed, in the Second Century we find hardly a trace of φιλέω (*phileō*). The New Testament writers and the early Christian Fathers invested ἀγαπάω (*agapao*) with a rich content.

In our Lord's time many petty feuds and personal animosities existed. It is to these that reference is made in the command: 'Love (ἀγαπᾶτε: *agapate*) your enemies' (Mt 5₄₄). It is clear that we cannot have a spontaneous fondness for those who have acted meanly and hurtfully towards us. It is the will and not the emotion that is involved in our Lord's saying. Though we may not have any liking for certain people, yet we can show such a spirit of goodwill and forgiveness as will appeal to the best in them. God does not treat us according to our deserts. In fact it is His sacrificial love on the Cross that has won so many who were in rebellion against Him. Even so must the Christian disciple act if Christ really lives in him (Gal 2₂₀) and is 'magnified' in his body (Ph 1₂₀).

This kindly concern for others will find expression in prayer. 'Pray for them', said Jesus, 'that persecute (διακόντων: *diakontōn*) you' (Mt 5₄₄). This **verb** is found in the papyri in reference to 'pursuit' by a lion. However viciously our enemy may act toward us, still it is our duty to pray for him. Our supreme example is Christ on the Cross (Lk 23₃₄). In a parallel passage to Matthew's we read: 'Pray for them that despitefully use (ἐπηρεαζόντων: *epereazontōn*) you' (Lk 6₂₈). This Greek word is found in the papyri with the meaning 'insolent conduct'. It implies a sense of pleasure which others have in molesting their enemies. In the only other passage in

the New Testament where it occurs it means 'to libel' (1P 3₁₆).
We are to be 'perfect' or, as the Aramaic version puts it, 'all
embracing in our love'—Mt 5₄₈; for God is kind to all (Mt 5₄₅).

This love will further express itself in service. In early
times couriers in Persia (and later elsewhere) carried important news from one stage to another across the country.
Post-horses were also employed. These messengers had a
right to compel a Jew to carry his baggage or his message one
mile. Simon the Cyrenian was a case in point (Mt 27₃₂). He
was compelled (ἀγγαρεύω: aggareuō) to carry the Cross.
Whenever a Roman enforced this duty, Jesus instructed His
disciples to go an extra mile.

This principle applies to (a) *Prayer*. We not only pray for
ourselves, but add our enemies to our prayer-list. (b) Our
approach to others. We shall be kind not only to our friends but
to the ungrateful and unlovely. Our forgiveness will be un-
limited and our patience all-enduring. (c) Our *Service*. We
will relate our Christianity not only to our own congregation
but to the great and troubled world outside.

Twenty

'HE TOOK THEM IN HIS ARMS'
(Mark 10₁₆)

THE Greek language has about sixteen different words to
describe the varied stages of infancy, childhood and youth.
Βρέφος (brephos) is the new-born babe (1 P 2₂); νήπιος (nēpios)
the suckling. Though παιδίον (paidion) can be used about a
servant, it denotes a little child and was applied to the infant
Jesus (Mt 2₈). It is the word referring to the little girl of
twelve in Mk 5₄₁. An old diminutive παιδάριον (paidarion)
is found only in Jn 6₉. The papyri reveal that this word could
be used about a schoolboy and also about a young man 'who
can drag on shore the magic fish that is to supply the safeguard
for his marriage'. Hippocrates states that παῖς (pais) 'in-
cludes all the stages from infancy up to twenty-one years of

age'. Νεανίσκος (neaniskos) is used about the rich young ruler (Mt 19₂₀₋₂₂), the 'young men' who 'will see visions' (Ac 2₁₇) and 'the young men who have overcome (νενικήκατε: neni-kēkate) the evil one' (1 Jn 2₁₃). This designation suggests youthful maturity even up to over thirty years of age. 'In the narrative of the Gospels', says Dr B. E. Warfield (see *Dictionary of Christ and the Gospels*, p. 304, vol. I), 'there is brought into contact with our Lord every stage of childhood and youth from the cradle to maturity; the baby on its mother's bosom (Lk 18₁₅), the little child, boy (Mk 9₂₄) and girl (Mk 7₂₅), children of a larger growth (Jn 4₅₁) (Lk 8₅₁) and the maturing youth (Lk 7₁₄, Mt 19₂₀).' In contrast with the Pagan contempt for baby girls and with the slaughter of the Innocents we see how Jesus Himself was tenderly cared for and grew into maturity without the stain of sin. Irenaeus truly says: 'Jesus passed through every age, becoming an infant for infants, thus sanctifying infants; a child for children, thus sanctifying those who are of this age. At the same time He became to them an example of piety, righteousness and submission; a youth for youths, becoming an example to youths and thus sanctifying them for the Lord.'

The tenderness of His nature is beautifully reflected in His attitude to children. He evidently loved to take them in his arms, laying his hands upon them and blessing them (Mk 10₁₆). 'Εναγκαλίζεσθαι: (enankalizesthai) comes from two words which literally mean 'To take into the curve of the arms or embrace'. The many allusions to children in the Gospels reveal how Jesus rejoiced in their company and closely observed their ways (for instance, Lk 11₇; Mt 7₉, ₁₁; Mk 9₁₇₋₂₇). The miracles which He performed on behalf of little ones unfold the compassionate nature He possessed. Expressions like 'mine only child' (Lk 9₃₈), 'The only son of his mother' (Lk 7₁₂), 'my little daughter' (Mk 5₂₃) and 'Children'—or 'boys' as we would say to young men—(Jn 21₅) reveal the affectionate nature of Jesus.

A little child was represented as a type of the children of the Kingdom. (1) One of the most striking features of an infant is its utter *helplessness*. Everything must be done for a baby. Unlike the lower animals which reach maturity much more quickly than 'a human being, the child has a longer period of dependency. Likewise, we have no means whereby we can save ourselves:

> *Nothing in my hand I bring,*
> *Simply to Thy Cross I cling;*
> *Naked, come to Thee for dress;*
> *Helpless, look to Thee for grace.*

Even Paul confessed that he was 'less than the least (ἐλαχιστότερος: *elachistoteros*) of all the saints' (Eph 3₈).

(2) The child is RECEPTIVE. Seldom does he refuse sweets and cakes, prizes and parties. His mind is open to new ideas. Curiosity leads him into a new world. (3) *Imagination* lights up that world. (4) *Wonder* makes living a thrilling thing to him. Wordsworth watched the daffodils 'tossing their heads in sprightly dance' and added:

> *They flash upon the inward eye*
> *Which is the bliss of solitude*
> *And then my heart with pleasure fills*
> *And dances with the daffodils.*

Similarly, the believer, who accepts the gift of Christ, as humbly as a little child receives his gifts, is introduced into a world full of delight and thrilling with new possibilities. It is significant that the Wesleys' 'Conversion Hymn' begins: 'Where shall my wondering soul begin?' As the child walks in an enchanted country where anything may happen, so to the sincere believer magic gates open. He

> *Laughs at impossibilities*
> *And cries: It shall be done.*

Twenty-one

'RESTORE SUCH A ONE IN THE SPIRIT OF MEEKNESS'
(Galatians 6₁)

'BRETHREN, if any man be overtaken in a trespass', says Paul, 'ye which are spiritual restore (καταρτίζετε: *katartizete*) such a one in the spirit of meekness' (Gal 6₁). This Greek **verb** literally means 'join together'; and it is one of the most picturesque words in the New Testament.

(1) A POLITICAL TERM, meaning to reconcile contending factions. Paul had it laid on his heart to bring to an end all estrangement among church members. He was greatly troubled, for instance, over conditions existing in the Galatian churches. 'If ye bite and devour one another, take heed that ye be not consumed one of another.' Two Greek words are used here δάκνω (daknō) ; καταφάγω (kataphagō) Gal 5₁₅, which were applied to vicious dogs. He gives lists of sins which include sexual vices and the worship of false gods, sins of faction like self-seeking and jealousy, and sins of appetite like drinking bouts and revelry. These all destroy the spirit of fellowship in the Church.

(2) A FISHERMAN'S TERM for 'folding' the nets and having them ready for use. The word also stood for 'mending' nets (Mk 1₁₉). Many a lapsed member of a congregation has been 'restored' and equipped to make the church a greater agent for winning others. 'Saved to serve' is a much-needed slogan in these days when the Communists are so alive to their duty to enlist others in their cause.

(3) A SURGICAL TERM for setting fractured bones (Gal 6₁). Just as the human body cannot discharge its functions efficiently when a bone is out of place, so the church is handicapped when some of its members have lost their contact with Christ. They may be amiable in many ways, kindly in disposition, but they lack that indispensable power to make them forgiving and sacrificial. The lack of prayer severs the line of communication between the soul and God. Until a person is brought into living contact with God, the Holy Spirit cannot adorn his life with the beauty of holiness. If he is to win others, he must be winsome himself.

(4) A MILITARY AND NAVAL TERM. It was used by Polybius in reference to 'supplying' an army with provisions and 'manning' a fleet with men. The Acts of the Apostles gives us a glorious picture of an avalanche of evangelism. Men and women were equipped with spiritual power, and though they were ordinary people, through the Holy Spirit they did extraordinary things. There are lapsed men with rich gifts and great possibilities who must be 'restored' to the Church.

Twenty-two

'BEAR YE ONE ANOTHER'S BURDENS'
(Galatians 6₂,₅)

WHEN we turn to the Epistle to the Galatians Paul makes two statements that seem contradictory: (*a*) 'Bear ye one another's burdens' (Gal 6₂); (*b*) 'Each man shall bear his own burden' (Gal 6₅). The significance of two different Greek words enables us to harmonize these statements.

(1) 'Bear ye one another's burdens.' The Greek word for 'burden' here is βάρος (*baros*), which literally means something that presses on a person. It is found in the papyri for 'a burden of oppression' and 'a burden of taxation'. It is used about the exhausted condition of the labourers in the vineyard who bore the BURDEN and scorching heat of the day (Mt 20₁₂). Modern society with all its social services is a happy illustration of this brotherly relationship. Christians are called to bear the burdens of all unprivileged people—the millions of illiterate, hungry and superstitious heathen; the displaced multitudes who are helpless refugees; the oppressed coloured people; the weak-willed victims of gambling, drink and immorality; the lonely rich, the feeble aged and the mischievous adolescent. Every Church needs a vigilance committee to be alert to social injustice.

(2) 'Each man shall bear his own burden.' The word here (φορτίον: *phortion*) literally means 'something carried'; it is used metaphorically of a ship's cargo. The RV Marginal Reading is 'load'. Xenophon mentions it regarding a man's shoulder-pack. Lightfoot thinks that the application of the metaphor here may be to a soldier bearing his own kit. The Christian must discharge his obligations.

We all have the load of our own responsibility to bear. We have to be obedient to our conscience and exercise right judgment. This we cannot delegate to others. Each man is responsible to God for the use which he makes of his time and his money, of his influence and his skill—in a word, of his whole life. Neither can he evade the responsibility of making up his own mind. Pilate tried to wash his hands of Christ as he appealed to the crowd: 'See ye to it'; but nevertheless, he is stigmatized as a guilty man. Parents must bear the responsibility of bringing up their children 'in the nurture and fear of the Lord'.

(3) The Greek word μέλω (*melo*) was used about a father's care of his child. This is the very word employed in the great injunction, 'Casting all your anxiety upon Him, because He *careth* for you' (1 P 5₇). Underlying all our responsibilities and enabling us to bear our own loads is the help of One who really cares.

Twenty-three

'I WILL GIVE YOU REST'
(Matthew 11₂₈)

ONE of the surprising features about Christ's offer of 'rest' was that it was made by a hunted and homeless Man, Who had short-sighted friends and open enemies. Obviously the rest that He spoke about was not dependent on outward circumstances. Nor did it consist of a stagnant and cloistered existence. As Dr W. R. Maltby used to say: 'Jesus did not promise to cradle adult babies. He called people to poverty, danger and death.'

The picture which He gives us is of two toiling animals, ripping open the stubborn soil amid the heat and glare of the pitiless sun and plodding up and down the whole day. 'Come unto Me, all ye that labour and are heavy laden, and I will give you rest. Take My yoke upon you. . . . My yoke is easy and My burden is light' (Mt 11₂₈₋₃₀). There are a few Greek words which are translated 'rest' in the New Testament. ῎Ανεσις (*anesis*) implies the relaxing of chords which had been strained. It is found in a papyrus in reference to 'relief' from taxation. It is often contrasted with trouble. Paul had no rest ἄνεσιν (*anesin*) in his spirit because he did not find Titus in Troas (2 Co 2₁₃). A second Greek word—ἀνάπαυσις (*anapausis*)—implies cessation from labour and refreshment for

further work.   It is used about giving rest to the soil by sowing
a lighter crop.   Paul employs it in reference to the way his
heart was 'refreshed' by the arrival of some friends to see him
(1 Co 16₁₈).   The rest that we experience in Christ in this
life is temporary; but in heaven where life is not bounded by
time there is to be a permanent rest.   We see thus the contrast
between ἀνάπαυσις (*anapausis*) and κατάπαυσις (*katapausis*).
The latter emphasizes the permanent nature of the rest.
'Let us give diligence', says the writer of the Epistle to the
Hebrews, 'to enter into that rest' (κατάπαυσιν: *katapausin*),
which is lasting blessedness (He 4₁₁).   The author of this
epistle also speaks of 'a Sabbath rest' and refers to the rest of
God after the Creation.   Augustine (in *De Civitate*) compares
the days during which the heavens and earth were created
with the ages of the world: and as the Seventh Day brought
about the completion of the Creation, so man's existence in this
world is consummated in an eternal Lord's Day.

Jesus referred to those 'that labour (κοπιῶντες: *kopiontes*)
and are heavy laden' (πεφορτισμένοι: *pephortismenoi*).   The
reference is to heavily loaded beasts which draw ploughs,
chariots or wagons.   Κοπιάω (*kopiaō*) means to do toilsome
work; φορτίζω (*phortizō*) was used about a heavy load which
had to be pulled by an animal.   It is very suggestive to recall,
too, that it was this word which was employed about a barge
that remained dangerously low in the water because of the
heavy load of merchandise on it.   How true is this today of
those who are burdened with a sense of guilt (with all its
psychological effects), massive anxieties that crush the heart
and dreadful fears that harass the mind.   To all such Jesus
offers rest.

How is this heavenly kind of rest found?   How can people
live serenely in the midst of a troubled world?   Jesus suggests
three ways: (1) The *mind* must accept the *Fatherhood of
God*.   The writer of St Matthew's Gospel informs us that just
before Jesus issued this gracious invitation to find rest He was
thinking of the Father (Mt 11₂₅₋₂₇).   As His Son, it is His
privilege to unveil the ineffable glory of the Divine Fatherhood.   'Learn of Me' (ἀπ' ἐμοῦ: *ap' emou*), said Jesus.   The
whole life of Jesus reflected the calm faith which He had in His

Father. As we trust in the love of God, there is no room for anxiety, fear or sorrow. (2) The *heart* must realize *the sense of the Divine presence*. 'Take my yoke (ζυγόν: *zugon*) upon you.' Just as a young, nervous animal, chafing at the bit and bridle, is steadied and calmed by being yoked beside an old and experienced one, so the fearful, discouraged or troubled person can face the worst and loneliest and most thronging duties refreshed in spirit and revived in heart because Christ is yoked beside him. (3) The soul finds rest, not only when the mind accepts the Fatherhood of God and the heart realizes the presence of Christ, but also when *the* WILL *is consecrated* to the accomplishment of the Divine purposes. 'In His Will is our peace', said Dante. The happiest people are those who are reflecting the sunshine of the love and joy of Jesus into the lives of others.

Christ's yoke is 'easy' (χρηστός: *chrēstos*). This word would be more correctly translated 'kind' or 'useful'. The word is found in the papyri with the sense of 'excellent'. Christ's yoke is the best of all yokes—so easily adjusted, so kindly in its effect and so useful in its purpose. Under it the heaviest burden seems light, for there is One beside us Who assumes the major share of the load and exalts our thoughts to the privileged purpose of saving the world.

But this rest is not given to them that labour and are heavy laden unless they respond to the call: 'Come (*deute*) unto Me.' This **verb**, which is frequently used in Homer and the lyric poets, is translated 'Come ye after (Me)' in Mt 4₁₉. Every believer can appreciate the words of Walter Rauschenbusch:

> *My troubles seem but the pebbles on the road,*
> *My joys seem like the everlasting hills,*
> *All my fever is gone in the great peace of God,*
> *And I pass through the door from Time into Eternity.*

Twenty-four

'BE OF GOOD CHEER'
(John 16₃₃)

'GOD loveth a cheerful (ἱλαρόν: *hilaron*) giver', said Paul (2 Co 9₇). The English word 'hilarious', of course, is derived from this Greek word, which in turn is from ἵλαος (*hilaos*), an old term meaning 'propitious'. Another form of the word is used in Ro 12₈: 'He that showeth mercy with cheerfulness' (ἐν ἱλαρότητι: *en hilarotēti*).

In the matchless parable of the Prodigal Son we read that 'they began to be merry' (εὐφραίνεσθαι: *euphrainesthai*). 'Luke is our principal witness', says Dr Alex. Findlay (in his book *Jesus, as they saw Him*), 'to the fact that Jesus not only tolerates the gaiety of simple souls who laugh, dance and sing boisterously when they are happy, but joins in with a disregard of dignity which reflects the merry heart of God.' On the other hand, the rich fool can only 'TRY to be merry', as the **tense** implies (Lk 12₁₉). He knows nothing of the real source of spiritual revelry.

The joy of Jesus was like a well in the inner stronghold of His heart, when the most malicious foes besieged His life. It consisted of more than a happy temperament or high spirits. 'In the world ye shall have tribulation', he announced, 'but be of good cheer (θαρσεῖτε: *tharseite*), I have overcome the world' (Jn 16₃₃). This Greek **verb** is used only by our Lord. Even in the solitary instance of its employment outside the Gospels it is the Risen Christ Who says: 'Be of good cheer, for as thou hast testified concerning Me at Jerusalem, so must thou bear witness also at Rome' (Ac 23₁₁). Θαρσέω (*tharseō*) is a deeper and richer word than εὐθυμέω (*euthumeō*) which also means 'cheerfulness'. This latter **verb** is found in the Epistle of James (5₁₃): 'Is any cheerful? Let him sing praise.' Θαρσέω (*tharseo*) might be freely translated 'put a cheerful courage on'. There is a solid foundation for optimism.

Indeed, Jesus usually gave some reason why His friends should take courage. There are a few instances worthy of our notice. (1) In the passage quoted above (Jn 16₃₃) Jesus bids us be of good courage because of *His victory over the world*. The **pronoun** ἐγώ (*ego*) is emphatic and the **verb** νικάω (*nikaō*) is always used of spiritual victory in the New Testament. The Book of Revelation is a magnificent illustration of this theme. What a story of triumphant rejoicing is set forth in that remarkable book!

(2)   Jesus bade His disciples 'Be of good courage' when *He assured them of His abiding presence*. The disciples in Peter's boat were battling with a strong wind and tempestuous waves. They were 'distressed (βασανιζομένους: *basanizomenous*) in rowing'. This Greek **verb** literally means 'to test by rubbing on the touchstone', then to elicit information by methods of torture. It was used in the papyri about the torturing of slaves. Later it meant the suffering resulting from being tested. As Jesus approached the struggling disciples, they were afraid of the ghostly figure; but He calmed their fears by saying: 'Be of good cheer; it is I; be not afraid' (Mk 6₅₀).

(3)   On another occasion Jesus mentioned *forgiveness of sins as a ground of cheerful courage* (Mt. 9₂). No doubt, according to the crude theology of that time, the shaking paralysis which troubled the young man was regarded as a divine punishment for sin. It must have been a miserable experience for the lad to know that he was a moral outcast and that the stern old Pharisees who gazed at his pitiable condition had a contempt for him. Like a shaft of sunlight illuminating a previously darkened room was the tender and compassionate look of Jesus at this boy. The lovely words: 'Cheer up, My son, thy sins are forgiven thee' must have been as a balm to his wounded soul. The heart which is at peace with God is flooded with an unconquerable joy.

Twenty-five

'FAITH IS THE ASSURANCE OF THINGS HOPED FOR'

(Hebrews 11₁)

IN all realms of life hope sets the tune for the march of progress. Its value is emphasized by a poet like Milton:

> *What reinforcements we may gain from hope;*
> *If not what resolution from despair.*

The hopes of men are often shattered. Heber says that they

> *fluctuate o'er this changing scene*
> *As false and fleeting as 'tis fair.*

But the New Testament word for hope (ἐλπίς: *elpis*) represents something more massive, virile and enduring than the mere expectation of good. Was Tennyson thinking of such a quality when he sang of 'The mighty hopes that make us men'? Paul links up hope with God. It is this foundation which establishes it amidst the tempestuous waves of discouragement, difficulty and distress. Indeed, Paul likens hope to a helmet (1 Th 5₈). It enables a man to face up to the insidious assaults of the evil one and, of course, it helps to prevent him 'losing his head'!

In a magnificent affirmation, the writer of the Epistle to the Hebrews says: 'Faith is the assurance (ὑπόστασις: *hupostasis*) of things hoped for' (He 11₁, RV). The Greek word literally means 'what stands under anything'; and it implies a steadiness of mind which keeps one firm. It has a legal significance. An authoritative translation (in *The Vocabulary of the Greek New Testament*: Moulton and Milligan) gives us this rendering: 'Faith is the title-deeds of things hoped for.' Just as the possession of title-deeds of property is a guarantee that such property—though it may be far away—legally belongs to the purchaser, so the possession of faith is an indubitable assurance that what God has actually promised can at once be claimed by the believer as his very own. Our forefathers had good reason to say that they could read their title clear to mansions in the sky. Dr Westcott points out in the verse which we are considering: 'The order (ἔστιν δὲ πίστις: *estin de pistis*) shows that the object of the writer is not to give a formal definition of faith, but to bring out characteristics of faith which bear upon his argument. The general scope of the statement is to indicate that the future and the unseen can be made real by faith. Things which in the succession of time are still "hoped for" as future have a true existence in the eternal order; and this existence faith brings home to the believer as a real fact.'

It is obvious that there is a ring of assurance about the biblical conception of hope. The Christian never merely hopes in the sense that a person hopes that next summer will be a dry one. He is firmly convinced about the future inheritance because he has already received the first instalment of his inheritance in the Resurrection of his Lord and in the gift of the Holy Spirit in his heart. Paul actually affirms this: 'The Spirit is the earnest (ἀρραβών: *arrabōn*) of our inheritance' (Eph 1₁₄). This Greek word was borrowed from the famous commercial nation of the Phoenicians; and it signified the first instalment of a payment which would finally be paid in full. Lightfoot says: 'It must be observed that the expression is not ἐνέχυρον (*enechuron*) "a pledge", but ἀρραβών (*arrabōn*) "an earnest". In other words, the thing given is related to the thing assured—the present to the hereafter—as a part to the whole. It is the same in kind.' As we live amidst material things and are confronted by temporal values, we can only imagine what the essence of the future life will be. But, when Christ gives us the Holy Spirit with all the wealth of spiritual experience which this implies, we have a first instalment of the quality of life which awaits us. Our heaven is already begun below.

This is in harmony with a phrase in the Epistle to the Romans: 'the first-fruits (ἀπαρχή: *aparchē*) of the Spirit' (Ro 8₂₃). The Spirit is, so to speak, the first-fruits of a harvest to be reaped in a future glorified life. Yet, we must not overlook the implication that as the earnest-money is only a small part of what will afterwards be paid, so the present possession of the Spirit is only a small fraction of our future endowment. It is of interest to note that ἀπαρχή (aparchē) was used in the papyri to signify 'the birth-certificate of a free person'. We too can claim our full sonship in the next world, as we have been certified by the Spirit. Another picture can be brought before us in regard to ἀρραβών (arrabōn). This Greek word in a slightly different form meant an engagement ring—a pledge of marriage. So we have in the above verse in Ephesians a strong ground of hope—the Holy Spirit is given to us not only as a first instalment of a rich reward but also as a pledge of a glorious life of felicity in union with Christ in the eternal world.

The word for 'hope'—ἐλπίζω (elpizō)—is sometimes translated in the AV by the **verb** 'to trust'. The RV adheres to some form of the **verb** 'to hope'. The Greek word is usually followed by one of three **prepositions**. (i) 'Εἰς (eis) (in) which indicates the direction of hope. This preposition is found, for instance, in 1 P 3₅ where the holy women of the Old Testament are cited as having hoped in God. (ii) 'Επί (epi) (on) suggests the ground on which hope rests. Take for an example Paul's advice to Timothy: 'Charge them that are rich in this present world, that they be not highminded, nor have their hope set on (ἐπί: epi) the uncertainty of riches, but on (ἐπί: epi) God Who giveth us richly all things to enjoy (1 Ti 6₁₇). The risen Christ is a solid rock on which to base our hope of immortality; all other suggestions are as shifting sand. (iii) 'Εν (en) (in) suggests the sphere in which the hope is implanted; and this is nothing else but Christ.

In his massive argument on the Resurrection (1 Co 15), Paul lingers over the appalling condition of the man who has no hope beyond the grave. Commenting on 1 Co 15₁₉, Dr W. F. Howard says: 'The order of the Greek words favours the RVm rather than the text. Probably Paul's meaning has best been brought out in the rendering: "If we are men that have had our hope in Christ in this life and nothing more", then we are most to be pitied of all men, because our hope in Christ has raised us to such a height of confident expectation only in the end to be dashed ruthlessly to the ground' (*Abingdon Commentary*).

The records of the lives of heathen people unfold a pathetic misery in the presence of death. Frequently we read of 'eternal farewells'. Very commonly used were the letters NFFNSNC over tombs. They represented the first letters of the Latin words 'Non fui, fui, non sum, non curo' ('I was not, I was, I am not, I do not care'). Contrasted with such gloom we find triumphant Christian inscriptions like this: 'Prima, thou livest in the glory of God and in the peace of Christ our Lord.'

Twenty-six
THEY 'THAT ARE FALLEN ASLEEP'
(1 Thessalonians 4₁₄)

PAUL uses many striking metaphors about death and the life to come. 'To die is gain' (κέρδος: *kerdos*), he says (Ph 1₂₁). This Greek word signified originally the financial profit of a business man. We are reminded of Dr A. T. Robertson's reference: 'To die is to cash in both principal and interest, and so to have more of Christ than when living.'

When writing to Timothy, the apostle makes another illuminating statement: 'Christ Jesus Who abolished (καταργήσαντος: *katargēsantos*) death' (2 Ti 1₁₀). This Greek word literally meant 'to render inactive'; then 'to make sterile'; and later 'to paralyse or render powerless'. In a figurative sense, it means 'to abolish', and is found no less than twenty-five times in the Pauline epistles. It is used of the 'coming to nought' of the world rulers. They will be overthrown (1 Co 2₆). Christ has devitalized death. It ceases to have any effect. 'Jesus awakens the daughter of Jairus (Mt 9₂₅) and the youth of Nain (Lk 7₁₄) as if from ordinary sleep. The life which to outward appearance had ceased, had only been withdrawn from the body, and could be reunited with it at the Divine Word'. (E. F. Scott in 'Dict. Christ and the Gospels : Hastings'.)

Consistent with this lovely view of death is Paul's statement in 1 Th 4₁₄: 'Them also which sleep (κοιμηθέντας: *koimē*-

thentas) in Jesus will God bring with Him.'   Though some translators would consider this **verb** to be **1st aorist passive**, and others the **middle voice**, J. H. Moulton says that there is a faint **passive force** in most of the instances of this word. Even the RV hardly does justice to the original in the rendering: 'They that are fallen asleep.'   It is possible to translate the phrase: 'Those that have been laid to sleep by Jesus.' Our Lord gives His beloved rest, just as a parent tenderly puts a tired child to bed and tucks him in.   The sleeping appearance of a dead body suggests the metaphor of sleep; but in sleep the self is alive, the brain is often busy and there comes a happy awaking.

Dr Swete said that it needed a voice from heaven to reveal such a beautiful beatitude as that in Rev 14₁₃: 'Blessed are the dead which die in the Lord . . . that they may rest (ἀνα-παήσονται: *anapaēsontai*) from their labours' (κόπων: *kopōn*). The former word (ἀναπαύω: *anapauō*) is a technical term in agriculture for resting land by sowing light crops on it.   Κόπος (*kopos*) is to be distinguished from other words for 'labour' and 'toil'.   It signifies not so much 'exertion' as 'exhaustion'.   It is translated 'pain' in Rev 21₄; and Paul uses it about the 'weariness' which he experienced in his apostolic journeys. There will be active service in heaven: to be idle perpetually would be boredom.   The servants of God will have their joys enhanced as they are appointed to

> those great offices that suit
> The full-grown energies of heaven.

Twenty-seven
'THE TIME OF MY DEPARTURE IS AT HAND'
(2 Timothy 4₆)

PAUL has a lovely word for death (ἀνάλυσις: *analusis*) in his last known letter (2 Ti 4₆).   It is (i) a SEAMAN'S WORD— 'unloosing' a ship from its moorings.   It gives us a thrilling vision.   Death is the beginning of a glorious voyage.   All lovers of John Masefield's references to the sea know how he

revelled in 'the wheel's kick', 'the wind's song' and 'the grey
dawn breaking'.   Death does not suggest a gloomy river Styx
but the great calm ocean of life in fellowship with God.

> For though from out our bourne of time and place
> The flood may bear me far,
> I hope to see my Pilot face to face
> When I have crossed the bar.

(ii)   Ἀνάλυσις (analusis) is a PLOUGHMAN'S TERM, meaning
'unloosing' a weary team of animals after a toilsome day's
work.   Paul had proved himself a gallant toiler; he passed
through peril, toil and pain.   Soon he would enjoy refreshing
release.   As a tired animal, set free in a field after an exhausting
day, does not usually lie down but canters about in the sheer
delight of freedom, so the rest of heaven will not mean absolute
inactivity.

(iii)   Ἀνάλυσις (analusis) is a TRAVELLER'S WORD, signifying
striking or unloosing a tent and continuing the march.   There
are many stages along the journey of our spiritual knowledge.
What progress was evident in Peter's life from timidity to gallant witness-bearing, from proud assertiveness to humble
obedience!   Endless new discoveries and surprising develop-
ments await those who pass with Christ through the dark
gorge of death up to the sunlit hills of heaven.   One day we
shall be like Jesus (1 Jn 3₂).

(iv)   Ἀνάλυσις (analusis) is a PHILOSOPHER'S WORD, implying the 'solution' of a problem.   'A dead child', said
Augustine, 'knows all that has puzzled the sages.'   Mysteries
of undeserved suffering, the prosperity of the wicked and the
death of some young talented life will all be cleared up when
'heaven's morning breaks and earth's vain shadows flee'.*

The Greek word which is translated 'mansions' (μοναί :
monai) in the lovely verse in Jn 14₂ can mean 'halting-places'
or 'stations' on a journey.   It would then suggest (a) stages of
glory along the heavenly road.   Our growth in spiritual
knowledge and our increasing capacity for appreciating the
splendour of the spiritual world can signify a series of endless

---

* The exposition of *analusis* was published in *The Christian World*, to the Editor of which
we are indebted for the use of the material here.

delights. (*b*) Some writers dwell on the fact that μονή (*mone*) originally meant 'a seat by the wayside' and then a resting-place; so the homely paraphrase has been suggested, 'In My Father's house there are many chairs'. There is an intimate sense of fellowship in the picture. (*c*) Μονή (*mone*) is the same word which is translated 'abode' in verse 23; and it is more likely that it means permanent dwelling-places rather than temporary halting-places. The imagery reminds us of the Eastern custom of combining different branches of the family in a single home, many dwelling-places being included in one spacious family residence. The main emphasis is on the fact that Christ, as a thoughtful and gracious host, goes earlier to that lovely spiritual world to make arrangements for His guests, and that there will be adequate room to receive all in His heavenly home.

Our Lord's words: 'I go to prepare a place for you' (ἑτοιμάσαι τόπον ὑμῖν: *hetoimasai topon humin*) (Jn 14₂) contain the very same **verb** which is used in two other Gospels about Jesus sending Peter and John to make ready a place for the Passover meal (Mk 14₁₂₋₁₆; Mt 26₁₇). There is a peculiar beauty about the words in the Fourth Gospel (Jn 14₃) which, translated literally, would read: 'I shall take you along (παραλήψομαι: *paralēpsomai*) to My home'.

'Now we see in a mirror in a riddle: δἰ ἐσόπτρου ἐν αἰνίγματι: *di esoptrou en ainigmati* (1 Co 13₁₂): but then face to face: now I know in part; but then shall I fully know (ἐπιγνώσομαι: *epignosomai*) even as also I have been known fully' (1 Co 13₁₂ RVm). There is all the difference between looking at a friend through the blurred reflection of a metal mirror and seeing him face to face. 'The suggestion is', says Dr. James Moffat (in his N. T. Commentary), 'the truths of God cannot reach us here and now except over our shoulders, as it were'. In that future life we shall know Christ, we shall know the past and we shall know one another. Love with its precious fruit of joy and communion will never fail.

> *There all the ship's company meet*
> *Who sailed with the Saviour beneath*
> *With shouting each other they greet.*

Twenty-eight

'LET NO MAN ROB YOU OF YOUR PRIZE'

(Colossians 2₁₈)

ON account of the widespread interest in the athletic contests in Greece we are not surprised to find references in the New Testament to these games. A few words are relevant here. Writing to the Colossians, Paul says: 'Let no man rob you of your prize' (καταβραβενέτω: *katabrabeuetō*)—Co 2₁₈. This forcible Greek term suggests the action of an umpire who disqualifies a competitor for a technical breach of rules. Even though the athlete has run in the race, some arbitrary condition having not been complied with, he fails to win the prize.

The preacher has a great theme here. (1) THERE IS A PRIZE TO BE WON. Though it used to be thought that the two Greek words for 'crown' had a distinctive significance (στέφανος (*stephanos*)—a crown of victory; διάδημα (*diadēma*) —a royal crown or diadem), Moulton and Milligan point out that the distinction cannot be pressed too far. We do find, however, in a papyrus that στέφανος (*stephanos*) was used about a golden crown that was sent to the Emperor Claudius by a gymnastic club of Nomads for his victory over the Romans. There was a peculiar glory associated with the winning of such a prize at the athletic games. When Xerxes was marching into Boeotia and heard that the Greeks were at the same time continuing the games, he asked in astonishment what prize they were contending for. When he was informed that it was a crown of olives, he replied: 'Amazing! What kind of men have we come to do battle with—men who contend not for gain but for glory?' In the first Book of his *Odes* Horace refers to the heroes of the Olympic Games being raised 'aloft to join the Gods'. Innumerable honours awaited the successful athlete on his triumphant journey home. Pindar wrote an ode in honour of one who brought glory to his city (Camarina):

Glory great, O Camarina, brought he to thy peopled town;
Six twin altars duly decking at the festival most high,
Where, mid sacrifice of oxen in the five days' contest vie
Car and mule and flying courser; and his triumph brought thee fame;
For thy new town's praises mingled with his father Acros' name.

We can thus appreciate Paul's phrase, 'finishing his course with joy'. For the Christian, it is no fading wreath of parsley or pine leaves, but a crown of everlasting life which is his glorious prize. This quality of 'life' (ζωή: *zōe*) denotes the highest blessedness.

(2) AN EFFORT IS NEEDED TO WIN THE PRIZE. 'I press on (διώκω: *diōkō*) toward the goal unto the prize' (βραβεῖον: *brabeion*)—Ph 3₁₄. Paul's eye is on the great destiny, to which God calls him. In another place he refers to the need for worthy living because God 'calleth you into His own kingdom and glory' (1 Th 2₁₂). Again, our lives must be disciplined. 'Every man that striveth in the games is temperate (ἐγκρα-τεύεται: *egkrateuetai*)—1 Co 9₂₅. The Olympian athlete had to go into training for ten months before the contest. He was most careful about his diet. Once a day he would rub oil on his body in the Gymnasium, practise the most strenuous exercises and bathe his limbs. No wonder Paul said to Timothy 'Exercise (γύμναζε: *gumnaze*) thyself unto godliness' (1 Ti 4₇). Unfortunately, there are many today who are included in the category mentioned in 2 P 2₁₄: 'having a heart exercised (γεγυμνασμένην: *gegumnasmenēn*) in covetousness.' We have to run with doggedness (δι' ὑπομονῆς: *di' hupomonēs*) 'the race that is set before us' (He 12₁). There is also involved 'the laying aside of every encumbrance', just as the athlete discarded his clothes in order to make the maximum effort.

What is meant by 'the sin which doth so easily beset (εὐπερίστατον: *euperistaton*) us' (He 12₁)? There have been various explanations due to the fact that the Greek word is not found elsewhere. (*a*) Chrysostom adopts the rendering: 'Easy to be put off or avoided' from the sense of περι-ίστημι (*peri-istēmi*) in 2 Ti 2₁₆. But, as Westcott points out, the compound could not have lost the 'i', therefore it must be derived from στατός (*statos*). This sense does not suit the imagery of

the passage.   (b) 'Popularly-supported' or 'admired of many'.
This is the view of some Greek writers.   But a Christian is not
unduly troubled about the popular conception of sin.   (c) The
best translation is 'close-fitting' or 'easily entangling'—an
image from trailing garments.   The Vulgate has 'circum-
stans nos peccatum' ('the sin standing around us').   Εὐπερί-
στατος (euperistatos) can be divided into three parts: στατός
(statos) is used of anything standing; περί (peri) would suggest
that it was placed around the person; and εὖ (eu) would
imply how very easily sin hinders us in the Christian race.
If we are surrounded by a cloud of witnesses, we are also en-
circled by sin.   In the original instance, apostasy was the
great sin.

(3)   Even though we run the race WE MAY BE DISQUALIFIED.
'Let no man rob you of your prize', said Paul.   We have already seen the significance of καταβραβεύω (katabrabeuo).
Paul has the same idea in mind when he says: 'I buffet
(ὑπωπιάζω: hupopiazō) (bruise) my body, and bring it into
bondage: lest by any means, after that I have preached to
others, I myself should be rejected (ἀδόκιμος: adokimos), not
standing the test' (1 Co 9₂₇).   The lesson is obvious regarding
people who belong to God: 'Let him that thinketh he standeth
take heed lest he fall' (1 Co 10₁₂).   We may travel a long way
through the wilderness of this world and yet be denied the
privileges and joys of our heavenly Canaan.

Paganism has no hope: Happy is the Christian athlete who
can say: 'I have fought the good fight (ἠγώνισμαι: ēgōnismai), I
have finished the course, I have kept the faith'; for he sees 'the
Lord, the righteous Judge' about to give him 'the crown of
righteousness' (2 Tim 4₇₋₈).

Twenty-nine

'BRANDED WITH THE MARKS OF JESUS'
(Galatians 6₁₇)

THERE is a well-known metaphor which is charged with
spiritual significance: 'I bear branded (βαστάζω: bastazō) on
my body the marks (στίγματα: stigmata) of Jesus' (Gal 6₁₇).

These marks tell their own story. Flogged and stoned, experiencing hunger and thirst, his brow furrowed with anxiety for the Churches and his body scarred with the wounds of enemies, it was a miracle he was alive at all. Like a veteran soldier, he gloried in his scars.

Various explanations have been made regarding the source of this metaphor. (i) *The use of a charm.* In the papyri there are frequent references to the custom of wearing a particular amulet associated with a god. This is supposed to act as a charm against hostile powers. Though very similar language to Paul's is found in a charm of the third century, his reference is hardly to this custom. (ii) *The tattoo of a soldier.* The marks of his commander were pricked into the skin in colouring matter. This also seems improbable. (iii) *The branding of a slave.* The symbols of a heathen deity were often so marked on the body. Ptolemy Philopater compelled the Jews to be branded with the ivy leaf, which was the emblem of the god Dionysius. Herodotus makes reference to a slave who found refuge in a temple and there received on his body the marks of a god. Thenceforth he was immune from arrest. These στίγματα (*stigmata*) implied absolute ownership. Wherever the slave wandered or whatever disguise he might adopt, the brands marked him out as belonging to a new master. Similarly, Paul had his stigmata. He rejoiced to be called the slave of the Lord Jesus. He was bought with a precious price. Others might discuss his authority, the Judaizers might question his claims, but he himself knew that his scars and wounds authenticated him. Today people look wistfully to professing Christians to see the marks of ownership—self-renouncing love, unconquerable joy, Christlike forgiveness, quiet courage and a regard for the welfare of others. The power to witness is found in intimate fellowship with Christ. Tyro was bought by Cicero as his slave; and he became his secretary. His master became so fond of him that he eventually liberated him.

Δοῦλος (*doulos*) is used over a hundred times in the New Testament. Paul and Peter, James and Jude in their Epistles speak of themselves as being 'bond-servants' of Jesus Christ. They all rejoiced in being 'the living tools of God'. Paul gloried in being freed from the slavery of sin. He became the

Lord's freedman.   Even our Divine Master 'emptied Himself,
taking the form of a slave, being made in the likeness of men'
(Ph 2₇).   There are three characteristics of a slave.   (i) He is
his Master's property.   Long ago slaves were bought and sold
like cattle.   The word 'talent' reminds us that the ability to
do certain things particularly well is a gift from God to be
used to the utmost for Him.   (ii) *A slave receives no pay*.*
Though it is true that great will be our reward in heaven if we
faithfully follow Christ, yet it is clear in the New Testament
that anything that we shall receive will be of the nature of a
merciful gift from God.   All the labourers in the vineyard
received the same wage.   The bond-slave of Christ has to do
without the pay of visible and immediate success, as well as
without appreciation from others.   (iii) *A slave obeys his
master's commands*.   He was defined by Aristotle as 'a live
chattel' and 'a live implement'.   He had no rights.   A suggestive word (*ὑπακούω: hupakouo*), which literally means
'listen attentively', is found in He 5₉.   Real waiting on God
involves a sincere willingness to hear His voice and obey His
commands.   In the same context we find the expression *νωθροὶ
ταῖς ἀκοαῖς (nothroi tais akoais)*, 'dull of hearing' (He 5₁₁).   It
means making no effort to hear, or lacking in concentration.

On the other hand, a New Testament writer uses the word
παρρησία (parrēsia).   We can 'draw near with boldness' (*meta
parrēsias*—He 4₁₆).   It literally means 'telling everything'.
Nero's freedman, Pallas, would not lower his dignity by speaking to his slave; he intimated his wishes by a nod or by writing.
Nor would he allow his slaves to address him.   In amazing
contrast to this restriction, we have the freedom of speech of
the children of God (Ro 8₁₅).

* For the expansion of this exposition see Dr A. H. McNeile's delightful book *Disciple-
ship* (S.P.C.K.).

Thirty

'EVERY GOOD GIFT AND EVERY PERFECT BOON'

(James 1₁₇)

THE crowning attribute of our Heavenly Father is that He is the giving God (Ro 8₃₂). We have already observed the significance of Paul's use of χαρίζομαι (*charizomai*), which originally meant to act in a gracious manner and then to forgive. There are three Greek words denoting 'gift' which are worthy of notice. They can be applied *to our* Lord.

(1) A GODLY GIFT. Δωρέα (*dorea*) is invariably used in the New Testament about a spiritual or supernatural gift. For example, 'If thou knewest the gift of God' (Jn 4₁₀). It is the word found in the papyri for 'the Emperor's beneficium to the soldiers', and the services of 'an honorary physician'. It was this word which Paul used as he broke into a spontaneous ascription of praise to God for His 'unspeakable gift' (2 Co 9₁₆). This gift was (i) useful; (ii) costly; (iii) thoughtful. Therefore it was greatly appreciated.

(2) A GOODLY GIFT. Δώρημα (*dorēma*) is found in what was probably a quotation from an ancient hymn where it is translated in the RV by 'boon' (Ja 1₁₇). The **adjective** τελέιος (*teleios*) is applied to it. This word for 'boon' is used by Paul for the gift of righteousness and reconciliation (Ro 5₁₆). The gift of healing and pardon for souls distressed and disintegrated is surely an opulent one!

(3) A GRACIOUS GIFT. Χάρισμα (*charisma*) has a variety of applications in the New Testament; but underlying all the instances is the idea that whatever we receive from God is a gift wholly due to His love and not to any merit of ours. The gift may relate to a merciful deliverance from some terrible ordeal in answer to the prayers of others (2 Co 1₈₋₁₁); or to the realization of a fellowship which would be fruitful in encouragement and instruction (Ro 1₁₁); or to some special capacity in the believer which is due to the power of the Holy

Spirit and which is received purely for the common good of the community (Ro 12₆; 1Co 12₄, ₉, ₂₈, ₃₀, ₃₁).

The gracious attitude of God is crowned with the glorious gift of salvation. Χάρισμα (*charisma*) is used in the familiar words: 'The wages of sin is death; but the free gift (χάρισμα: *charisma*) of God is eternal life in Christ Jesus our Lord' (Ro 6₂₃). We have here a threefold contrast: (i) Two CLAIMANTS, God and Sin. (ii) Two CONDITIONS, God offers the free-gift (χάρισμα: *charisma*) of His gracious and purposeful fellowship: Sin offers pay for fighting against God. The Greek word ὀψώνιον (*opsōnion*) was used in the papyri and is found in Lk 3₁₄ and 1 Co 9₇ with the meaning of a soldier's allowance. The metaphor, therefore, has reference to warfare rather than to slavery. (iii) Two CONSEQUENCES. He who repents and turns to Christ receives 'the life of the ages' (Weymouth; Ro 6₂₃). He who obeys sin receives as his pay nothing less than insensibility to spiritual things, moral apathy and estrangement from God.

In that great passage in Mt 7₉₋₁₁, where Jesus refers to the willingness of our Heavenly Father to give good gifts (and even the Holy Spirit; Lk 11₁₃) to those that ask Him, Dr Alex. Findlay reminds us that the Greek word for 'give' really means 'make a present of' (*Jesus and His Parables*, p. 102; Epworth Press).

But if a gift is offered, there must be the willingness to receive it. 'Receive ye (λάβετε: *labete*) [the gift of] the Holy Ghost', said Jesus in the upper room (Jn 20₂₂). There are several Greek words for 'take'. The **passive term** suggests taking as you take the light of the morning. The militant word is to take as you wrest something from the unwilling. But there is a third term which is to take from a friend who kindly offers a gift. Λαμβάνω (*lambanō*) is used about our Lord's gracious offer of the bread at the Last Supper: 'Take (λάβετε: *labete*), eat; this is My body' (Mt 26₂₆).

As the **article** is not in the Greek (preceding 'Holy Spirit') in Jn 20₂₂, the emphasis is on the energies which originate in the Third Person of the Trinity: *lambanō* has three significant relationships: (i) The receiving of Christ (Jn 1₁₂); (ii) the receiving of the Holy Spirit (Ac 1₈); and (iii) the receiving of the crown of life (Ja 1₁₂). We receive the gift of the Holy Spirit just as we breathe in the life-giving oxygen from the air. Such a believer becomes spiritually robust. The man who needs more heart in his religion must have more religion in his heart.

PART THREE

The Study of the Word of God

UNLESS the preacher has an interleaved Bible—an invaluable source of reference—he would be well advised to keep a note-book in which to jot down impressions and suggestions during his daily reading of his Greek Testament. What a storehouse of material he will soon accumulate for his sermon-preparation! Let the writer stress again the great reward that comes to him who carefully reads the Greek; and even when on holiday a minister who follows the Scripture Readings in public worship will find his devotional life deeply enriched. Let us sum up certain points that should be noticed.

(i) THE ORDER OF THE WORDS. We note, for instance, that the word for 'therefore' (ἄρα: *ara*) is the second word in Ro 8₁. It links up the magnificent chapter about justification and assurance with all that is expounded in the preceding chapters. Again, we shall notice the emphatic 'I' (ἐγώ: *ego*) when our Lord makes a gracious offer of some gift (Jn 4₁₄). Once again, take as an illustration 1 Co 8₆: 'Yet to us there is one God' (ἀλλ' ἡμῖν εἷς θεός: *all' hēmin heis theos*). There were numerous statues of Roman, Greek and foreign deities in Corinth. The Christians, however, had only one God; 'but to us' is emphatic. Moreover, 'one Lord Jesus Christ' is mentioned in contrast to a local deity, 'one Lord Serapis'.

(ii) THE ARTICLE. The absence of it can be very suggestive. 'God hath spoken unto us in (a) Son' (ἐν υἱῷ: *en uiō*). Here the relationship rather than the personality of One Who is a Son is stressed (He 1₁). Compare 'THE prophets' in the same context. They are thought of as a definite body fulfilling a particular office in diversified ways; but the final revelation is mediated through One Who holds a unique relationship. The personality of the Son is mentioned later. Again, whenever the article is not found before the expression

'Holy Spirit' the emphasis is on the element of the new life and not on the Personality of the Holy Spirit (Jn 1₃₃). This revival of the human spirit is, however, the work of the Third Person of the Godhead. (See also 2 Co 1₂₂.)

(iii) THE GENDER. An interesting illustration is found in 1 Co 3₈: 'He that planteth and he that watereth are one' (ἕν: *hen*). It would seem as if Paul by using the **neuter gender** here wished to emphasize man's humble part in the scheme of things. The instruments are ONE THING—parts of a vast piece of machinery (as it would seem to us) which God has put into motion for the salvation of the world. This is in harmony with Paul's use of the metaphor of a slave, who had no rights and was regarded as 'a tool' of his master's.

(iv) THE TENSE. The significance of this can be seen in the words addressed to the rich young ruler: 'Sell (πώλησον: *pōlēson*) . . . give (δός: *dos*) to the poor . . . follow (ἀκολούθει: *akolouthei*) Me' (Mk 10₂₁). The two first **verbs** being in the **aorist tense** imply a single act; the third word being the **present imperative** suggests continuous following of Christ. Similarly, we observe the significance of the **perfect tense** in 1 Th 1₄: 'Brethren, beloved (ἠγαπημένοι: *ēgapēmenoi*) of God'. If it were **present tense**, the idea would be that God only loved them now; but the **perfect** brings out the meaning that God loved them in the past, before they embraced the Christian Faith, and His continuing love for them is realized in the present.

(v) THE MOOD. In our Lord's statement: 'How shall ye escape (φύγητε: *phugēte*) the judgment of hell?' the fact that the **verb** is in the **subjunctive mood** indicates that Jesus was asking a question rather than making a threat (Mt 23₃₃).

(vi) THE VOICE. Where it is used, the subject is specially involved in what is mentioned. For instance, φανερόω (*phanero-ō*), which is in the **active form** in Jn 21₁, suggests that the appearance of Jesus after the Resurrection depended on His own Will. He was pleased to manifest Himself. Paul says: 'Lay hold on (ἐπιλαβοῦ: *epilabou*) eternal life' (1 Ti 6₁₂). The use of the **middle voice** suggests, 'Get a grip on it for your own sake; you yourself are responsible.' It is of interest to observe that νοσφίζω (*nosphizō*), which literally means 'set apart', signifies in the **middle** 'to set apart for a person's own use' and thus 'purloin' (Tit 2₁₀). It is used about Ananias and Sapphira (Ac 5₂, ₃).

We can thus see how valuable and helpful can be the careful observation of the form of Greek words. Many a text can be enriched by some added emphasis to the truth that is enshrined in it. For instance, Paul speaks of the Jews 'who both killed the Lord Jesus and the prophets' (1Thess 2₁₅). The words in the Greek read: 'The Lord they slew, Jesus—as well as the prophets'. As 'Lord' was a title applied to God, the appalling nature of the crime is shown up in its worst light. 'Jesus' brings out the idea of 'a Saviour'. Hence the crucifixion was a dastardly atrocity. Then again, the observance of the singular 'fruit' (καρπός: karpos) of the Spirit as contrasted with the mutually antagonistic 'works' (ἔργα: erga) of the flesh, reminds us that there is a unity of character produced by the Holy Spirit, just as there is the same life producing all the fruit on an apple tree.

The distinction between ἄλλος (allos) and ἕτερος (heteros) is important. One is a positive and absolute word; the second is a comparative and relative term. The first suggests 'another' of the same sort; hence Jesus promised 'another (ἄλλον: allon) Comforter', that is One like Himself. The second term suggests 'another' of a different sort; hence those who are crucified beside our Lord are ἕτεροι κακοῦργοι (heteroi kakourgoi)—Lk 23₃₂. The Risen Christ appeared to His disciples 'in another (ἕτερα: hetera) form' (Mk 16₁₂). The word implies that a great change had taken place, as at the Transfiguration (Lk 9₂₉).

Some valuable sermon material can be gleaned by combining or contrasting picturesque words. Διστάζω (distazō), which is translated 'doubt' in Mt 14₃₁, literally means 'to stand at two ways, puzzled which way to travel'. Peter had his mind partly on Jesus and partly on the unstable sea; he was looking in two directions. Contrast this with He 12₂ where ἀφορῶντες (aphorōntes) implies: 'looking away from all that distracts and fixing one's gaze on Jesus'. Again, what a contrast there is between the two uses of καταφιλέω (kataphileō) (to smother with kisses) in (a) the father kissing the Prodigal

(Lk 15₂₀); (b) the traitor kissing Jesus (Mt 26₄₉)! Or, once again, link Mk 14₃₁ with Mt 26₄₀. Peter, who vehemently stated that he was willing to die by the side of (σύν: sun) Jesus, could not watch even one hour in His company (μετά: meta). Yet another contrast is seen in Jn 19₂₇ and Jn 1₁₁, where the same words εἰς τὰ ἴδια (eis ta idia)—'to his own things' ('to his own home')—are found. It is interesting, also, to contrast two aspects of our Lord's life in the words πλήρωμα (plērōma—'fulness') and ἐκένωσεν (ekenōsen—'He emptied Himself') in Col 1₁₉ and Ph 2₇ respectively.

Indeed, there is hardly a verse which we read in Greek which does not yield some treasure. For instance, we are not merely to 'render unto Caesar the things that are Caesar's', but—as the **verb** ἀποδίδωμι (apodidōmi) was used regularly for 'paying a debt'—we have a definite obligation to fulfil in that direction. The use of ἐδωρήσατο (edōrēsato) regarding Pilate's surrender of the body of Jesus (Mk 15₄₅) implies that he willingly gave it without extorting money. Mnason was an original (ἀρχαῖος: archaios) disciple and not merely an 'old' disciple (Ac 21₁₆).

The word ἄνωθεν (anōthen) in Jn 3₇ is ambiguous. It literally means 'from above'. It was used of tracing a river 'from its source', tracing the course of all things accurately 'from the first' (Lk 1₃), of the rending of the veil of the temple 'from the top to the bottom' (Mt 27₅₁), of our Lord's seamless coat that it was woven 'from the top' throughout (Jn 19₂₃). Though 'born anew' is a permissible translation, signifying that salvation is a radical and far-reaching work (rebuilding from top to bottom), yet John's use of ἄνωθεν (anōthen) suggests the rendering 'born from above'. Thus salvation is not merely self-reformation, but the coming down of new life and the reception of a heavenly gift.

One other observation we make in this direction. Until we have a new English version we shall have to notice carefully the words in our present versions. Take two instances. Peter exhorts his friends to be holy 'in all manner of conversation' ('all manner of living'—RV). This phrase represents a word ἀναστροφή (anastrophē), which means 'to turn upside down', 'to turn aside' or 'to turn hither or thither'. With

God's Word is like God's world—very rich, very varied and very beautiful. The famous preachers of the past were noted for their expository sermons. Though many modern translations are illuminating, nothing can set the heart of the preacher so aglow with delight as the discovery in the original language of some new presentation of an over-familiar theme. We must still preach on the great texts. We must still expound the glorious doctrines of our Faith. But often the problem is how to get the message across to the worshipper! The preacher will be helped to overcome this difficulty if he links his knowledge of God with his knowledge of human nature, and out of a diligent study of the truth he proclaims a living message with all the joyous passion of one who has discovered an old truth in a new setting.

He is a happy man indeed who can combine accurate exegesis with spiritual insight, an alert mind with a burning heart and a fresh interpretation of some glorious theme with a relevant application of it to the conditions of this troubled and challenging world. It was said of David Hill that he read his Greek Testament daily and found it to be a spiritual tonic and an intellectual treat. Nearly all his sermons were derived from readings and notes on the original language. May a similar study stimulate many other preachers to explore the spiritual riches of this immortal book.

INDEX OF GREEK WORDS

INDEX OF SCRIPTURE REFERENCES